Dream Horse

After success with Dream Alliance, Janet Vokes has continued to breed racehorses and hopes to find another champion. Her ambition now is to win the Cheltenham Gold Cup. *Dream Horse* is her first book.

JANET VOKES

with Jeff Hudson

Dream Horse

PAN BOOKS

First published 2019 by Macmillan

First published in paperback 2020 by Pan Books
an imprint of Pan Macmillan
The Smithson, 6 Briset Street, London EC1M 5NR
Associated companies throughout the world
www.panmacmillan.com

ISBN 978-1-5098-8604-3

All photographs courtesy of the author, except for page 4 top,
page 5 top and middle and page 7 © Gareth Everett / Huw Evans Agency
and page 6 bottom © Alan Crowhurst / PA Archive / PA Images

1 3 5 7 9 8 6 4 2

A CIP catalogue record for this book is available from the British Library.

Printed and bound by CPI Group (UK) Ltd, Croydon, CR0 4YY

Visit www.panmacmillan.com to read more about all our books
and to buy them. You will also find features, author interviews and
news of any author events, and you can sign up for e-newsletters
so that you're always first to hear about our new releases.

To Dream Alliance.
More than a horse, more than a winner.

Contents

Prologue

Kelly's Daughter

'But what if he can't do it?'

I couldn't hide my fear any longer. What were we doing here? What if I'd got everything wrong?

'He's going to be great, love,' my husband Brian reassured me. 'He's our boy, remember that. Look, there's the entrance.'

I looked over to where he was pointing. It may have been my first time at Newbury Race Course but I could read well enough and the sign above the door said 'Owners' Entrance'. That, funnily enough, was exactly what was printed on our tickets. I took a deep breath and we followed the rest of the crowd. We'd come this far, hadn't we?

All my life I've struggled to get myself noticed for what and who I am. As a young girl I was always 'Kelly's daughter'. When I started school I was 'Trevor's sister', even though I was ten times brighter than him. When I got married I became 'Daisy's wife'. That's what the village knew me as. Just once, just once I wanted to do something that nobody could take away from me. Something that got me recognized as a person in my own right. Me. Not some relative, not some bloke. Not some tradition.

And that horse out there in the parade ring at Newbury was my best chance of doing it.

Forget my nerves, I'd have fought through fire and water to see my boy's first race. He looked so beautiful. Chestnut all over apart from four near-identical white socks and a striking white blaze between his eyes. Whatever happened I loved him and I was grateful. He'd already given me so much. To be honest, he'd given the whole town and community a new lease of life. Wherever he placed, whatever he did, I would love him.

'But don't be coming last, now, will you, boy? Don't let me down,' I said. 'I don't want to go back to being just Kelly's daughter.'

1

Rag and Bone

Bert 'Kelly' Davies met my mother in the Potteries during the war. She's English, bless her, but we all have our cross to bear. Dad was pure Welsh stock, born in Aberbargoed and the eldest of four brothers. Why everyone called Dad 'Kelly', though, is anybody's guess. People said it was because he resembled an old family member with the same name who had been a bare-knuckle fighter in the Rhondda Valley. His father, my grandfather, was a miner who had scraped by but always put food on the table for them all.

As if Mum hadn't suffered enough with her nationality, she had a really hard upbringing in Stoke to boot. Her father worked in the Potteries but wages were low and she often went to bed hungry at night. No money, no real education and for a large chunk of her life no parents either. Her mother died and was buried on her fourteenth birthday. Her father passed eleven months later. Her older brother and sister had already flown the nest so Mum was left on her own and forced to find work to keep a roof over her head. She was just a girl, poor love.

In 1939, when war broke out, she was just sixteen and working in the Potteries like her father, but she soon moved to an ammunitions factory when she was old enough. She struggled by and ever so occasionally scraped together enough money to have a little night out as a treat. I've always admired the way she looked after herself during that time. She always said that with hard work you could get to where you wanted to be, regardless of your background or where you come from.

One evening, a few years later at a NAFFI dance, she met a young man serving in the Royal Air Force and they hit it off. He was about to be stationed in Egypt but they started writing letters to each other and, somewhere along the line, they became boyfriend and girlfriend. Dad couldn't bear his girl struggling on her own, but his Mum, my grandmother, was a bit more resistant. She wanted him to marry a Welsh girl. Regardless, he persuaded Mum to up sticks and move to Aberbargoed in south Wales where she would be closer to his family. She lodged with a young school teacher before moving in with Dad's family a few years later. They got married on Boxing Day 1946, when Dad was home for a few days on leave.

I don't know how you have a marriage when you don't see each other for months at a time. But they made it work and when my father was released from the RAF in 1949 they picked up where they'd left off.

Dad was a toolmaker and turner by trade, but the war changed everything. When he came back there was no work, so he did what everyone else in the Valleys did – he went down the mines. We lived in what is now the Caerphilly district of Monmouthshire, but just about that entire part of Wales was synonymous with the coal industry. It's what had fuelled the Industrial Revolution and by the 1940s it was still as important as ever, especially to the local area. Without it, the outlook for the Valley region would have been very grim indeed.

As, I'm afraid, it proved.

Aberbargoed then was nothing like it is today. When I was young you could have been born there and died there. You still could I suppose. It's just harder – and a lot less fun. Back then we had everything you needed for a full life. We had a hospital, we had a Co-operative, we had a fire station, we had a butcher's, we had a cinema, florist, baker's, several chapels, a church and a miner's institute, which housed a library and classrooms for the local junior school. Everything was there, we didn't have to leave the village at all. And I suppose a lot of people didn't because there weren't many cars in those days, and the Valleys is the Valleys. If you want to walk anywhere you'd better be bringing your hiking boots.

And it was all thanks to the pits. Dad worked down in Bargoed but there were collieries every which way you looked: there was Elliott's up the valley, there was Britannia, there was Oakdale, they were all around us. And what would we have done without them? You could trace every penny spent in the town back to the coal. It wasn't just the miners, you had the lorry drivers, the food suppliers, the doctors – so many industries depending on the coin from the pits. My father was the eldest in his family; his money came from digging, the same as his youngest brother. But the two in the middle were electricians and milkmen – whose biggest employers were, you guessed it, the collieries.

Once he'd been demobbed, my father and mother moved in with an old lady in Cwrt Coch Street. That's where I was born, number 10 Cwrt Coch Street. My brother Trevor came first in 1950 and I appeared three years later. Me and that boy, we're chalk and cheese now. He's quiet and reserved and I'm a bottle of fizzy pop. Don't know when to give up, don't want to neither. Growing up, though, kids are just kids. You just get on with things.

When I was six months old we moved to a self-contained ground floor flat at 141 Commercial Street. It was part of a purpose-built block of four, and had a kitchen, a little sitting room, two bedrooms and – quite posh for the time – a little bathroom. The rest of our family were still washing in a tin bath in the lounge and peeing outdoors.

It wasn't all luxury. My dad used to come home black

as your hat. They had showers at the colliery but my father preferred a bath. When he came home all you could see was his eyes. It used to give me nightmares when I was young. I thought the bogeyman was coming to get me. Until he spoke I'd be hiding behind my mother's skirts.

I loved our flat. The block was in the shadow of a beautiful stone-built tabernacle chapel but that's not what I enjoyed looking at. For me, it was the mountains front and back of the house.

People say we were deprived back then, but we weren't. I think kids today are deprived because they spend so much time in front of screens and on iPads and phones that they don't see the world. They don't get any fresh air, they don't get any exercise and they don't get to explore their imaginations. My god, if it wasn't a school day every child on the street was out from the early morning until we were told to come home. Even in term time you'd be hard pushed to find us in until it was dark. We'd do all sorts, of course, but at the heart of everything was the pair of mountains bookending our house.

Except they weren't *mountain*-mountains. They weren't made of mud or rock or granite and they never saw a blade of grass. They were slag heaps, plain and simple. But they were Snowden to us.

When you're digging down and down for years, not everything you bring up is going to be coal. All the detritus, all the slag, all the crap, it had to go somewhere and right then it was behind our flat and on the new tip out the front.

The machinery was a thing to behold. The buckets with the coal in would come up to the pit-top at Bargoed Colliery, go to the washery, and once everything worth extracting was extracted – basically anything they couldn't sell – the buckets would then carry the crap up to the winding house at the top of the old tip behind our flat. On wires like little cable cars the buckets would cross the main road via a big gantry and empty out on the new tip at the back of our flat. There were two wires across the road, one bringing the buckets up and one taking the empty buckets back down. That happened every hour of every day and those tips just got bigger and bigger and bigger. Which was fabulous for us.

Oh, the fun we had. People said the tips were an eyesore but to anyone under ten they were anything but. They were our playgrounds, our treasure islands, our everything. In the winter we were skiing on the Alps. You would jump on a tray and hang on in the snow for dear life and I swear Franz Klammer wouldn't have gone faster. In summer it was even better because that's when you could really hurt yourself. We used to make these carts – gambos we called them – out of floorboards and old pram wheels, drag them to the top of the tip and just bomb down. We had no brakes, no run-off areas, no adults supervising. It was bliss.

The tip at the back of our house was the biggest in Europe they said. I didn't doubt it. I swear it blocked out the sun some days. To the side of it was a school, not a small one by any means but you barely noticed it next to the slag giant next door. Between the two was an alley, about five-foot wide, that led to Bedwellty Church and its graveyard at the back of the tip. By the school there was a long, low-walled area full of slimy grey mud where the water used to come down off the tip. I remember my dad warning, 'You are not to play in the mud because you will sink and disappear.'

My mother said the same thing: 'Keep well away or all that will be left of you is your hat.'

Seeing as her words were falling on deaf ears she'd add, 'If you do anything outside the church God will see you. That's his house.' It meant we were always on our best behaviour when we went to Sunday school.

Come October and she'd take it up a notch. There was a magpie that came in our garden and Mum would say he worked for Father Christmas. 'You don't want to do anything that gets you on the Naughty List, do you now?' Of course we knew she was fibbing.

I don't think there was a parent in the village who didn't predict the same quicksand doom for anyone who set foot in the deadly sludge but of course we ignored them. That's what kids do. We lost a good many wellies in there but I don't remember any children disappearing. Not for want of trying, mind.

One of the other things the mums and dads were against was crossing the road. Cars were few and far between but double decker buses would travel from New Tredgar to Crumlin through Aberbargoed all day and they were massive. An encounter with one of those would only end one way.

Luckily we had options. There was a big pipe that went under the road. I say big, I wouldn't get through it now, but as a kid you could crawl through without touching the ceiling. It was damp, mind.

A load of water came up in the buckets with the slag and of course it just ran downhill as soon as it could. Without the pipe the road would have been flooded all the time, because it carried all the excess filthy water underneath. Which is exactly where we were playing. If our parents knew about it they'd have dragged us right out. It was ten times more dangerous than crossing the road.

Plenty of other people knew what we were up to. The slag heap workers found out first hand. During the school holidays we'd sometimes climb up our mountain and move all the crap around until we'd made a dam to trap the water. It would build up and up and after a couple of days there'd be a reservoir waiting for us. Then it was just a matter of waiting. You'd see the workmen coming out of their houses, walking down the road ready to man the machines at the slag heap. That's when we'd knock over the dam.

The sludge tsunami poured down the south face of

the mountain and of course the further the water went the faster it travelled and the more crap it picked up. If it hit any of the workmen they were drenched through and even if they managed to dry themselves they'd stink to high heaven all day. Great fun, amazing fun. Unless you were one of the poor souls trying to get to work.

Even with Mum and Dad working all hours, money wasn't exactly flush. Not that we were any worse off than every one of our neighbours. Each family made savings where they could with clothing and furniture and what have you, but with something as essential as food, hand-me-downs just won't do so most people had an allotment somewhere or other and my father was no different. He shared his with my grandfather and my uncle. You might move from one flat to another but that piece of land remained where it was. My brother Trevor and I weren't welcome there unless it was to help with the groceries. That land housed chickens, pigs, and every vegetable you could grow in that climate. We had eggs every breakfast, pork every Christmas and all the carrots and peas you could dream of. Although, to be honest, as a five-year-old, that wasn't many.

Growing up there were always animals around. Trevor and I would collect frogspawn in pots and wait for the tadpoles to grow. Dogs were the only ones in the house as well as one pure white budgie called Joey. The first dog I remember was Mitch. He was nasty, he would bite you as good as look at you. I was about six when he died and I can't say I missed him. I thought all dogs were like that until a few days later we found a visitor in our garden. It was a pretty little black thing, a bitch Trevor said, whippet-like in shape I suppose you'd say, and very skinny. Too skinny. I thought she was the most beautiful thing I'd ever seen.

She had a bit of rope around her neck so Trevor and I took her into the house.

'Dad, Dad, we've got a new dog!'

Oh, he took one look at that bitch and said, 'Shame you can't keep it.'

'Why not?'

'Well it's got a collar. It belongs to somebody, doesn't it?'

He told us to go out around the neighbourhood with the dog and knock on every door until we found the owner.

'Okay, Dad,' I agreed, glum as you like.

'Come on,' Trevor said, 'let's get it over with.'

I don't know who was the better actor, me or him. We took the dog out, as promised, we went down the alley towards the back of the school and then we sat there. And we sat there and we sat there. For two hours we didn't move. It was only when it was getting too dark to see that we traipsed home and said, 'Dad, we tried, we knocked everywhere, but we can't find the owner.'

'Fair enough,' he said, 'I suppose she'd better stay with us.'

I named her Judy after Judy Garland in *The Wizard of Oz*. She was a lovely bitch and she just got more beautiful. Unlike the peacocked preening rat over the road.

Mrs Jones, who lived opposite us, had a poodle. A right fuss she made of her, always primping and preening and carrying her when there was a spot of drizzle. It was her pride and joy. I thought she was a bit boring if I'm honest. I just didn't like the look of her, not compared to our beautiful Judy. When the poodle had puppies Mrs Jones didn't keep one. She sold them all off for a tidy sum. Which I thought was opportunistic because they were so dull. Why would anyone want one of those? Anyway, a few months later a stranger's dog ran into our garden when Judy was in season. I didn't know any of this business, all I knew was that a few weeks later I was told Judy was pregnant.

I felt like a mother myself. I watched over her as she grew and swelled, and started nest-building in her little area of the kitchen. When the big day came her puppies were all different sizes, all different colours. You wouldn't have known one was related to the next. Which I loved. To my mind they were ten times more beautiful than those boring dogs across the road with their identical faces and ways. And if they'd made a few bob at market, think what our beauties would fetch.

I went running over to my father and said, 'Dad, Dad – we're going to be millionaires!'

He said, 'How'd you work that out, love?'

'The puppies! We can sell them like Mrs Jones did with hers and be rich.'

'Oh, Janet,' he said and took my hand to stroke it. 'Her dogs are poodles. They're pedigrees.'

Like that meant anything to me.

'I know! Judy's are much better.'

'No, no, no, you don't understand. Our dogs are mongrels.'

I nodded, still happy as Larry. I thought mongrel was a breed.

It took me a while to accept that our puppies were worthless. Even longer to appreciate exactly why. Just because of their background and their parentage other people placed no value on them. Even though they were gorgeous and they were as strong and fit and happy as any mutt you've ever seen, they didn't have the right background for them to amount to anything.

'I'm sorry, love,' Dad said, 'that's just the way of the world. But remember – mongrels are excellent ratters and will be your best friend for life.'

'That's not right,' I said. 'Who cares where you come from? You've either got it or you haven't.'

Get me: six years old and a burgeoning class warrior. My parents thought it was funny, this little girl telling them how the world should be. I was six years old and I was already prepared to take on anyone who told me my

dog wasn't as good as theirs because it didn't have something called a 'pedigree'.

I had no idea I'd still be ranting about the same things
fifty years later.

My father knew all about pedigrees. Out on the bit of
land we called a back garden at the back of the flats he
had his own little business going on. He'd built a shed
and fixed a shelf all the way round the four walls. That
shelf was lined with cages, every one of them built by his
own hand, and in those cages were little budgerigars.
They were every colour you can imagine. Blues and
greens and yellows and all shades in between. They weren't
there for fun. We never had one in the house. He bred
them to show at competitions. He never competed himself. He was too shy and retiring for that, like Trevor I
suppose. Dad got his pleasure from breeding the perfect
bird and selling it on. It was like a science project for him,
or a maths equation. He would pair his birds up, mix-
and-match boys and girls and try and get the best
elements of each bird into a brand new one. My father
wasn't the most talkative man in the world but he tried
to explain the process as best he could. For the perfect
show budgie you need a certain depth of chest, the exact
length of tail and a richness of colour to make a judge
weep and my father would work really hard to combine
the best elements of what he had to try and get something
stunning hatching later in the year.

Whether he had the right words or not, he never minded letting me watch. I remember thinking, *It's like watching my mother cook.* It's all about having the right ingredients, not how much you've paid for them. You don't need to know which hen has laid an egg to make a nice cake. A bag of sugar from Fortnum & Mason and a bag from your corner shop will probably make your tea taste just as sweet. I think my dad understood that. He said to me, 'It's not about buying the best, it's about looking at what you've got and seeing what you need to improve upon it. After that it's a bit of a detective mission. You just have to find it.'

I loved to listen to the whys and wherefores but honestly, I mostly loved just seeing the eggs. Dad had all the nest boxes hanging by the door of the shed so he could stick his face in, lift up the lids and have a peep. The back garden was out of bounds from the point of breeding. When the eggs were laid he'd allow us another look then we were banished again until hatching. We would mark the days down on the calendar in the kitchen. Once the birds cracked out their shells and they were happy he'd lift us up and we were allowed to see them in their ugly, bald glory, then he'd shut the box and we'd not get another glimpse until they feathered.

Only then were we allowed to play in the garden.

I never really thought about it at the time, but my Dad spent his entire week down the mines in the darkness. It was no wonder that in his spare time he loved to play with colour and beauty. He was underground for 50 per cent of his life. The fact his pets could soar so high into the sky must have been his way of escaping. He would never have done anything for attention. Just knowing he'd created something special was all the reward he required.

When I was ten we moved about a mile down the road to the new Britannia housing estate and that was the end of the budgies. We lived on Hodges Crescent, a small street of twelve properties, and I finally had my own bedroom. The move also signalled the end of my academic ambitions. Or rather, the end of my mother's ambitions for me. I failed my Eleven Plus, much to her frustration. It was a narrow miss – so narrow they put me on the reserve list in case anyone dropped out – but significant enough for her to vent her disappointment any chance she got. Me, I wasn't too bothered. Aberbargoed Secondary Modern School was perfectly nice and I thrived there. The name of one school over the other didn't matter a jot to me. So when, at the end of the first year, I got a letter offering me a place at Bedwelty Grammar School, I didn't exactly jump for joy. My mother, on the other hand, was smiling like the Cheshire Cat that got the cream.

This is my chance, I thought. *This is my opportunity to make her proud.*

But, you know, the more I thought about it, the more

I realized I was settled at ASM. I had all my friends. What more could I want for? If I went to the grammar school it would be just out of snobbery, wouldn't it? I may as well be a stupid poodle and have people judge me on my hair. So I said, 'No. Thank you, but no. I'm staying at my comp.'

I thought my mother would never get over the disappointment.

Neither having a second-tier education nor being known as Trevor's sister impaired my progress. I passed every test the school threw at me. When I finished at ASM I enrolled at Crosskeys College in Newport for a course in shorthand typing, office management and bookkeeping. I didn't really have a masterplan. I just knew I had to make the most of any opportunity that came my way, however slim. Being a coalminer's daughter shouldn't hold anyone back but the truth is, for a lot of people it did. I was determined not to be one of those.

As time went on, I soon realized I hated college and found other things to distract me. I was coming out of Crosskeys one day, walking to the bus stop at Blackwood for the ride back home, when I heard the distinctive 'clip clop' of an old horse pulling a cart along the street. There was a bit of shouting as the horse came to a stop in front of us.

'Is that Brian?' one of my friends said. 'What *is* he wearing?'

'Go on, Jan! Get up there!' another boy shouted.

I looked at the person they were describing. He wore an old black donkey jacket with no sleeves, a bowler hat and a pair of wellies with his socks turned down over the top. Compo from *Last of the Summer Wine* could have been modelled on him. He was a sight to behold, no question.

But he was also my boyfriend.

Oh no, Brian, I thought. *Not here, not now. Not while I'm wearing a miniskirt.*

I waved the lad away and luckily he took the hint and carried on round the bend. A minute later I made an excuse to my pals and walked round the corner he'd taken.

'What are you like!' I said when I found him, beaming, by the horse. 'Behave, will you?'

'Come on, Jan, aren't you pleased to see me?'

'You know I am, Brian. I just don't want to flash my underwear in front of the entire street!'

Brian laughed as I took his hand and clambered up onto the double seat. There was a bit of a whiff, if I'm honest, but that's horses for you.

'Oh no,' Brian said, 'that'll be the manure I had in here this morning.'

'You what? You expect me to get onto a cart that's still warm from the crap it's been carrying?'

'Come on, Jan,' he grinned, 'how else was I going to pay to take you out tonight?'

Honestly, that man could have me in stitches every

moment I was with him. And he knew it. Seconds after promising to behave if I got in the cart, he clicked the horse to go, gave me a cheeky smile then yelled: 'Rag and bone! Rag and bone! Bring out your gear. Rag and bone!'

Oh, I could have died. I was mortified. But that's Brian for you. He was terrible, he was, always looking for the laugh. But you know what, that's what I liked about him. And, anyways, I'd done a lot worse to him the first time we'd met.

Much, much worse.

When I was fifteen, my best friend Maureen and I used to go to a dance in Bargoed on a Saturday night as there was no social life on the estate. Sometimes we never made it to the dance hall and would just sit by the bus stop and talk about school and boys. It was there that I noticed 'Daisy', as he was known, in the field opposite taking care of his horse every week. Not one to hang about, I liked what I saw and knew I needed an excuse to speak to him. So Maureen and I hatched a plan. It was the summer holidays and five weeks before I was due to start at Crosskeys. Maureen had a little sister who needed looking after while her mum was working so we decided to take her along to the field to feed Daisy's horse. It was the perfect excuse.

The day came and off we trotted to the field. I quickly spotted Daisy hobbling around with the horse over the way. It had a saddle on and everything. Maureen's sister was so excited and I'd never been that close to a horse before. I was about to get closer. Daisy noticed us watching and called over. 'Come on,' he said, 'don't be scared. He's not hurting anyone.'

We found our way round to the gate and made our way across the field. Only when we were a few yards away did I realize why Daisy was hobbling. He had one leg in plaster up to his knee. It didn't look comfortable. He laughed at my expression.

'It doesn't hurt much. Just gets in the way,' he said. Determined to make the right impression, I quickly started chatting away.

'Why does everyone call you Daisy?' I asked. 'It's such a strange name!'

More laughter. He did that a lot, I realized. 'It's a long story. My real name is Brian but everyone calls me that.'

Apparently, when nine-year-old Brian used to go up to visit his father at work on a farm, his Dad would say, 'Have you been kissing that Daisy Greenock again?' and Brian would get so embarrassed. So, as one of ten children, it became a name for his brothers and sisters to mock him with and somewhere along the line it stuck.

I said, 'How are you going for a ride with that leg in plaster?'

He said, 'I'm not going anywhere unless you help me now.'

This was my chance! 'Okay. What do you want me to do?'

'Number one: say hello to Doll.'

Doll was the horse.

'Number two: hold these and whatever you do, don't let go.'

He handed me the reins and no sooner were they in my mitts than he started to climb aboard. I'd never had anything to do with an animal bigger than a whippet but I thought, *How hard can it be?* I was vaguely aware of him putting his good leg in the stirrup. I say vaguely because I couldn't take my eyes off the horse. Her head was huge, the size of my body at least. She had eyes like tennis balls and long lashes. I never knew horses had lashes. Never occurred to me either way, to be honest. Brian was just about to cock his bad leg over Doll's back when suddenly those big eyes took on a menacing stare. That's what I saw anyway. Her giant nostrils snorted – fire for all I knew – and then my worst nightmare happened. She took a step towards me.

I stayed exactly where I was for precisely one second. Then as she took another step I took two backwards and then just dropped the reins completely. It's the worst thing I could have done. That was it. The horse was off.

With Brian dragged along behind it.

I don't know about Maureen's sister, but I definitely heard words that day I'd never come across before. I don't blame him, mind. He had one foot in the stirrup and the other waving around, the plaster bashing against every rock and stone in that field. I felt so bad. Afterwards Brian had to go back to hospital to get it all recast. I think I added about a week to his recovery.

When I told Maureen's mum later that day what had gone on she said, 'Oh, I'd stay away from him if I were you.'

'Why's that?'

'He's a wrong 'un that Daisy Vokes. Always in trouble for smacking this lad or that. Bad family, I reckon.'

I was shocked, to be honest. He hadn't seemed the sort. He was certainly a size. He never missed a meal, that much was obvious. But that smile of his. And the fact all he cared about was his bloody horse. Surely he wouldn't hurt a fly.

I couldn't sleep that night with worry. Nor the next. There was only one thing for it, I had to go back up to that field to see if Daisy or Brian or whatever he called himself was all right. If he wanted to have a go at me at least I'd be able to outrun him. Not that I felt it would ever come to that.

Approaching the field I nearly turned around twice. I could only imagine how angry he was with me. If someone had made a horse drag me around on my back I'd still be livid today.

I couldn't have been more wrong. If Brian was angry he hid it bloody well. We got chatting and he told me how his leg had been hurt in a car collision with a drunk driver. He told me he worked on the buildings before the accident. He told me about his family, his million siblings, he told me about his reputation and all. I didn't even have to bring it up. Yes, he was a big lad, and yes he could and had caused the odd bruise and broken nose here and there. But he wasn't a bully. In fact, the only people he'd ever had problems with were bullies themselves. In school he'd got picked on for being on the plump side. And because he was quiet, even much smaller boys would make him give them piggybacks and call him names. In the end he said, 'I just had enough, I snapped, and I turned round and gave them all a thump and no one ever bothered me again.' More than that, if he was in a situation when he saw a lad or lass being bullied, he'd intervene. With his fists. He said, 'I'm not proud about it but I'd rather the bully were lying on the ground than the people they were hurting.'

Apart from the smile – he's missing the odd tooth now – he hasn't changed in the fifty years since.

Everything Brian said that day made me like him more. The fact he was twenty-one to my fifteen just added to his exoticness. I wished and wished he would ask me out but sadly he never did.

Luckily, he had very good friends.

One day while I was up at his field one of the other lads who hung around with him sidled up while Daisy was busy in the stable.

'He likes you, y'know.'

'Are you sure?'

'He'd like to ask you out.'

'Really? Why can't he ask me himself?'

'You'll have to ask him that.'

So when he came back, I did.

'Daisy Vokes,' I said, 'what are you doing letting one of your mates ask me out for you?'

He couldn't even look at me. His shoes got the scrutiny of their lives.

'I was worried you'd say no.'

'What would it matter if I did?'

'Well, I'd be heartbroken, wouldn't I.'

'Just as well I'm saying "yes" then, isn't it?'

2

Jump in the Saddle

My father never took to Brian. The wrong pedigree I suppose.

That hurt, it did. Brian was my first crush and I would have loved to have brought him home and showed him off to my parents. They just didn't want me to be too serious over anyone at that age. Who knew where it was going to go but not having their support sort of helped push it in one direction. Exactly where they didn't want it to go.

We were going out and that was that. Not that it wasn't without embarrassment. Brian was – and still is – as shy as a mouse peeping out of its hole. But when he relaxes he's the biggest, funniest, friendliest bear of a man. I loved him, I knew that by the time of my next birthday. Nothing ever got him down – not his leg, not being bullied, being dragged around a field, being forced to go rag'n'boning to make a dollar. He always saw the bright side and he always saw the best in me. For a young girl with ambitions that was an aphrodisiac in itself. Not that I knew what an aphrodisiac was, I just knew I liked him.

My parents, like a lot of people, preferred to believe the worst about him cuffing this thug or that one. The version of the stories where he was a hero never entered their minds. Or they weren't prepared to listen.

The Brian I knew was determined and inventive. The cart he used to pick me up in at Crosskeys was his first. He'd always ridden horses but it was only when his injury stopped him working on the buildings that he'd scratched around for another career – and lugging stuff about in a cart seemed a likely alternative. If, that is, he found a cart.

One day he spotted the hay wain he knew he wanted about two-and-a-half miles from his house, somewhere over Gelligaer way. He walked there the next morning with his friend Maldwyn, asked if it was for sale, knocked the geezer down to three pound for the wagon, then walked all the way back.

Pulling the cart himself. With Maldwyn in the back.

I wish I'd seen it. This limping, lumbering bloke wearing a horse harness and dragging a two-wheeler behind him. He probably would have raised a fortune doing it for charity these days. But Brian just did what needed to be done. No fuss, no drama. Same as he's always been.

I knew nothing about horses but Doll was a beauty. A

brood mare, thoroughbred cross, Brian described her as. Whatever she was, she took to the cart and pulled him hither and yon selling on her own manure to allotments and gardeners as well as picking up and flogging metal and household scraps. I was impressed by his independent spirit. The only thing I was less keen on was him filling the cart with horse dung the second before I climbed aboard.

I wish I could have shared these stories with my parents but they weren't interested. That is, until the day Brian suggested we get married.

Of course I said yes.

Under the age of eighteen you need your guardian's legal permission to tie the knot so we decided to wait until after said birthday. We never asked my parents for permission because we didn't need to. Anyway, I knew what the answer would be from my Dad: 'Over. My. Dead. Body.'

It was the same old record every time. 'You're too young to get married', 'You should keep your distance'. I like to think my dad was just looking out for me, not wanting me to settle down too quickly with my whole life ahead of me, but as Brian and I reflect on nearly fifty happy years together, it's fair to say he was wrong. 'I can pick a winner,' I said, but Dad never trusted me. Not to have an opinion, not to decide anything for myself. So, on the Saturday after my eighteenth birthday, when I legally became an adult in British law, Brian and I got hitched.

It was a beautiful October day. My mother made the bridesmaid dresses and my dad even walked me down the aisle. That's a miracle for you right there. All Brian's family were there, my family was there, it couldn't have been much better. I just wished it had happened a year earlier.

At the end of the night when all the guests had gone home I said to Brian, 'I have a present for you.'

'Oh,' he said, embarrassed, 'I haven't got you nothing.'

'I think you have,' I said.

I made him sit down.

'Brian Vokes,' I said, 'you're going to be a dad.'

Oh, his face. He was over the moon. I'd known a few weeks and hadn't told a soul. I didn't want to distract from the wedding. But as soon as we were wed I could tell everyone. To a man, people were happy for us. Apart from one person.

My dad.

To say he hit the roof is an understatement. The names he called me. 'If I'd known you were pregnant I would never have walked you down the aisle.'

I said, 'What's the problem?'

He said, 'Sex before marriage is the problem.'

From that day he totally blanked me. When I went into the house, no matter what time of day it was, he would leave the room and go to bed. Midday on a Saturday, five o'clock on a Sunday, didn't matter. Off he'd toddle, not a word to me. I thought it was funny.

It wouldn't have mattered quite so much if I weren't living under the same roof. It had surprised us both when my parents said we could live with them once we were married, until we found a place of our own that was. I wanted to do it less than Brian – he's always been mischievous like that – but with his own folks giving their spare room to one of his newly-wed brothers, we quickly ran out of choices. Thank the lord it was only for a few weeks.

We were that desperate we'd have considered a hole in the road. When someone pointed us in the direction of an old house that belonged to the Salvation Army it wasn't far off. You wouldn't be allowed to live in it today. In 1971, mind, rules were a bit more flexible. We put down the deposit and two days later moved in.

God loves a trier and you had to be one to stay there. You're meant to move up in the world. We were definitely going in the other direction. For a start, there was no bathroom. We had an outdoor lavatory and a tin bath I'd fill with buckets of boiling water from the stove; we didn't have running hot water, we had to get a gas geyser to supply it.

There were three bedrooms but only one had a ceiling; in the other two you could see the rafters. And there were rats. Loads of them. You'd look out the back window some days and swear the garden was alive there were that many. They came down from the colliery and lived in the tip over the back.

The house was a funny shape. An optical illusion, really. From the street it was two storeys, straight up and down. But from the back it had another level. It was on such a hill that to get to the loo we had to walk down into a cellar then out the back door. Because we never owned the place we never developed the downstairs. That doesn't mean it wasn't used. I was about seven and a half months pregnant and I had gone shopping one day. Brian had left the house before me, to take our new spaniel Susie for a walk, but he wouldn't be long. I came home and he still wasn't in. *Okay*, I thought, *you just leave everything to me, will you*. Then I heard this noise.

Bang, bang, bang.

What the hell is that?

Bang, bang, bang.

It sounded like it was coming from downstairs but, given we backed onto a tip and an allotment, I didn't give it much thought. I just hoped it would stop before it gave me a headache.

Anyway, the banging continued so I thought, *I've got to get to the bottom of this.* I started walking down the stairs to the cellar and the noise stopped. I nearly went back up but I thought, *If it's an open window slamming in the breeze it's not going to shut itself.*

Down I went, step by step, totally concentrating on listening out for the noise. I was virtually tiptoeing. All my senses were focused on tracking down the source of irritation. Which is why I jumped out of my skin when the creature stuck its head around the corner. I was expecting rats at worse. Them I could deal with; them I was used to. But this was no rat. It was something much, much larger.

A horse.

Finding Judy wandering in our garden was a godsend, but not unheard of. Dogs run away all the time. But who the hell expects to find a bloody nag in their cellar?

I was still getting my breath when I heard the front door upstairs. Brian came trotting down, not a care in the world – but then he saw me sitting on the steps.

'Oh dear,' he said.

'"Oh dear" is right. Do you want to tell me what the hell is going on?'

It turned out he'd bought the horse for his brother for a knockdown price and had to store her somewhere while he went to sort out getting her tacked up on a local farm. The way he figured it, the horse would be gone from the cellar before I got back.

We laugh about it now but if the baby had popped out that instant I wouldn't have been surprised.

The whole business with my father was very disappointing. Mum had warmed to Brian but continued to tell me

I had broken Dad's heart by marrying him. If they had been half as wicked to my brother I'd have put it down to them being them. But that boy could have brought home a harem of women and I think he'd have got away with it. Years later I asked my mother, 'Why was Trevor always your favourite?'

She looked shocked. 'Don't say such a thing,' she said. 'You have no favourites with children.'

'Well, how can you come down on me like a ton of bricks for everything and he gets away with murder?'

'Oh, that's different,' she said. 'The truth is you were always going to be okay, weren't you? Whatever happens to you, you bounce back. But Trevor was shy, he needed my help, he was the weakest chick.'

No favourites among children she said, but when my son Dennis arrived in April 1972 my parents were all over him like a rash. They couldn't leave him alone. They showered him with gifts and clothes. It's like they felt guilty about their prior behaviour but they couldn't find it in them to say 'sorry'.

But then when I had my daughter Sasha the following year they didn't have as much time to see her as they worked full-time. I used to go down to visit them every Sunday instead, sometimes with the kids and sometimes without. Dad even became less hostile to Brian over the years – it's funny how time can heal things!

Brian's parents were the total opposite of mine. If I'd had horns and a tail they'd still have put up with me for the sake of their grandkids. If we turned up at Brian's mum and dad's without Dennis and Sasha there'd be havoc. 'What are you doing coming here without the nips?' They were fantastic grandparents and couldn't have done enough for us.

My children were born a year and a half apart. If I could have squeezed a pair out in twelve months I would have. I wanted to have two children, but I also wanted to get it over with, then get on with my career.

After Crosskeys College I'd got a job with – surprise, surprise – the National Coal Board in Cardiff. I did all right, my skills fitted the role and the supervisor said I could go places if I kept it up. 'Greater things' he said I was destined for, and I liked the sound of that.

The problem was, life wasn't sustainable. I was leaving first thing in the morning and getting home late at night. At home I had a little baby who I never saw. So I gave up the job and looked for something closer to home. My mother alerted me to a position in the local sewing factory where she worked so I applied and took a job on the finishing section. It didn't require much brain power to stitch a few hemlines and that and my shorthand and office management skills were overkill, to be frank, but at least I got to see Dennis and then, later, Sasha. And, as I told myself, it was only for a short while. Just till the kids were at school. Then I'd go back and pick up my career where I left off. I had to prove my old supervisor right, now, didn't I?

Of course, I never did. I regret it to this day. I met some lovely people at that sewing factory but a chimp could have done what I did. Every day that passed I'd think, *There must be more to life than this. I swear I'm destined to do something more.* Then I'd go home, play with the bairns, make tea and forget all about my ambitions until the next mind-numbing shift.

You wonder if everyone thinks the same way. If other people feel trapped in their lives. Brian always seemed happy enough whatever he was doing. After his leg came out of the plaster he'd gone back to the buildings and was there a good few years happy as larry. Then he went on the coal lorries for a private contractor. Didn't seem to bother him what he did as long as there were horses waiting at the end of the day in the field.

Brian and his horses were a constant of our marriage. He always had one, if not for work then for pleasure. He'd be gone entire days sometimes just riding in the hills. I envied him really. The man who left the house was totally different from the chap who returned. It wasn't just the sweat on his brow or the reddishness of his cheeks, there was a glint in his eye that said, 'I've touched God today.' I think people who ride horses feel that all the time.

Me? I never picked up the reins. That's not to say I'd never touched a horse. Brian was always on the lookout for a new horse and when he found one advertised in the paper he took me along to view it. Not for the company and definitely not because I knew anything about them, but because he wanted to see how the thing took to a rider.

'Right,' he said when we got there, 'you jump in the saddle and I'll hold her steady.'

After what had happened the day we met, I didn't know whether to trust him. If he'd taken his revenge and slapped the mare's backside I couldn't have complained. But I found my way into the stirrups and he led the girl out into the field. I'd never really thought about horses that much. I certainly didn't realize how big they were. Until you're on one, you don't appreciate the scale of them. In the saddle I cleared Brian's head by four or five feet. It's like being king of the world up there.

I can't say riding ever appealed to me. I'd go down to the allotment where Brian had his stables, I'd brush the horses and clean out the hay while Brian was riding but that was enough for me. Being in their company ticked my boxes. Brian was another level. I bought him a horse once from the free ads. The kids were young and money was tighter than ever so he'd decided he couldn't justify the expense of renting a field and all that so he gave up his horse. I respected him for that but watching the change come over him was mortifying. He'd go up to one of the farms every so often and there was a woman there who'd let him ride hers, but it wasn't the same as owning. He never said anything, never complained, but you'd catch him when he thought no one was looking and he had a face as long as one of his nags. So I looked in the papers and found something to cheer him up.

The gentleman who owned it had bred it to ride himself, but he had been in a car accident and the thing had never been touched. The horse had been living on the mountain when we came along. A sensible person would never have gone through with the purchase. The horse was just too much of a handful. But Brian loves a challenge. We got the horse back to the stables and he worked on it day and night. In the beginning it went for him the second he popped his face round the door. But Brian never gave up. He would sit in the stable talking to it and talking to it until in the end it would do anything for him. He was ever so grateful but that's what marriage is about, isn't it? You can't always do things on your own.

I think the key to lasting more than five minutes in a relationship is having some time to yourself and some other times that you share with your other half. Brian loved his horses and as much as I helped out, they were his thing. Not being into riding meant I never really got my feet under that table. On the other hand, I've always loved my knitting and crocheting. He'll wear what I make but he won't join in. And that's fine by me.

But we always like to have at least one hobby we can do together. Believe it or not, when we were newly-weds, one of those hobbies was fishing. You really find out about a person when you're freezing your wotsits off on a muddy riverbank waiting for a creature you don't even know is there to bite on your hook. I can't say I was ever going to go out there after marlin but I enjoyed it at the time. As ever when the pair of us are together, we had a laugh. A few other anglers took it dead serious, but if you can't enjoy yourself then what's the point of living?

At the end of the day, though, fishing is a bit hit or miss for me. I thought, *I want to be doing something where I've got more of a say in the outcome.* I also wanted to do something with creatures that had a few more legs. Four more, to be precise.

'Brian,' I said one day, 'we're going to Crufts.'

'What?' he said. 'I bet those tickets aren't cheap.'

'I'm not going as a punter, am I? I'm going as a breeder.'

'Of what?'

Honestly, that man sometimes.

I said, 'I'm going as the breeder of a champion dog.'

'What do you know about breeding?'

'Nothing yet. But I will soon enough. And you're going to help me.'

'Oh crap . . .'

3

We're Going to Crufts

'What on earth are you talking about, woman?'

Oh, he's always had a way with words.

'I said, you watch me Brian Vokes. I'm going to breed a dog that's going to win medals.'

'What sort of a dog?'

'A whippet.'

'Lucky we've got one then . . .'

It's true we had a whippet but before that we had Susie. Lovely and dopey she was. But we didn't buy her as a plaything. We bought her as a working dog. When we weren't fishing Brian and I loved to go out with the guns and see what we could catch for supper. I had a .410, which is a small rifle, and he had a 12 bore, more your classic size and shape. We used to go to the local farms all round the area, take the dog and she'd flush out whatever was in the undergrowth, and if we potted something she'd run and fetch it. A lot of people think it's cruel but a lot of those same people still end up eating the identical thing. How do they think it got on their plate? Suicide?

We didn't always have a car when the kids were young but when we did we would travel further afield and test ourselves out against the terrain every which way. We enjoyed ourselves in west Wales so we bought a holiday caravan there and got friendly with a couple on a farm. They liked shooting as well and their land was ripe for it. A few times when they went away they invited us to 'farm sit', which was a dream come true. I think we'd have loved that lifestyle if circumstances had been different.

The guns of course were kept all safe and tidy. You don't take risks with kiddies around, do you? We didn't even leave the dogs alone with the bairns. As soon as we got in and comfortable Brian would dismantle the weapons and hide them away. Even if a ten-year-old did find them they wouldn't know what to do with them. As for the cartridges we used, they were stored right at the other end of the house.

Then of course the government started to crack down on the sport. In the early 1980s they brought in all these new regulations supposedly to make families safer. It was a joke really. They said you had to have a steel cabinet screwed to the wall. That's the only place your gun can be kept.

One minute my son and daughter are oblivious to where we keep our rifles. I'm not even convinced they knew we had any. The next minute we've a bloody great box showing them exactly where. They'd need to be able to break into the cabinet, and no way would they ever have the key but you don't want to take the risk. So sadly we gave up our licences and sold the guns.

We weren't going to let red tape ruin our fun, though, so we decided to take up coursing. This is only for rabbits and the like. What you do is you send a dog, usually a pointer or a reacher or a greyhound – basically something bloody quick – into the undergrowth. They ferret out the rabbit or whatever, chase it, catch it and bring it back to you. Sometimes you need to put it out of its misery, but often the prey has already gone.

We couldn't find one of those sprinters and Susie wasn't quick enough so we got a whippet called Gypsy. I found her in the paper, a beautiful white thing. She was fast as lightning and to my eyes gorgeous. When you have a whippet you then start noticing them everywhere. But mine didn't look exactly like those in the books and magazines. It wasn't noticeable at first – there was certainly nothing wrong with her – but I came to realize the ones that were winning prizes and recognition were all a bit tidier here and there. So I looked at her one day and thought, *No offence, beautiful girl, but I can improve on you.*

That's when I said to Brian I was going to breed a winner. My mind was made up. You couldn't have stopped me at gun point. I became a bit obsessed, I think.

It must have been my father and his budgies in the back of my mind because suddenly all I could think about was getting a slightly better version of the dog I already had. I didn't know the first thing about it, mind, so I went through the papers, I asked around and eventually I went back to the lad I'd bought the dog from.

'Do you know good stud dogs?' I asked.

He put us in contact with a few people, some money changed hands, the deed was done and a while later we were the proud owners of a gorgeous litter of puppies. Oh, it was fabulous. They were like little velvet mice, all warm and wriggly. And of course, like a typical mother, I thought they could all win a beauty pageant.

'I could make champions out of any of these.'

'I don't doubt it,' Brian said. 'But that's the favourite right there.' He picked out a little bundle of brown and white joy.

'Are you sure? She's very small.'

'You won't get better than this.'

I trusted my man with horses so I was happy to be led on the dogs.

'Hello, little lady,' I said, and that's the name we kept. Her brothers and sisters we sold and then it was down to me.

'What's the next step then, Jan?' Brian asked.

'That's the problem,' I said. 'I don't have a bloody clue.'

*

If you got talking to Brian you wouldn't believe it but he's very shy. Very, very shy, in fact, especially with strangers. I was spending my life down the library researching and researching but that was only getting me so far. I said to him, 'We're going to have to go to a show and speak to some people in the know.'

'Oh. I'm not sure I like the sound of that. Can I stay at home?'

'No, you bloody can't. Come on.'

There was a show up in Tredegar in the leisure centre. A dog needs to be older than six months to enter and Lady was younger so there was no danger of me getting carried away and throwing her in at the deep end. But I might as well have done for how embarrassed Brian got. We arrived at the venue with our little puppy and I saw a group of people over the way with similar dogs, just a bit older.

I said, 'Look, they've got whippets, let's say hello.'

Brian said, 'You can't do that, Jan! You don't know them.'

I said, 'Watch me.'

So I take my puppy and I start talking and the next thing you know they're all welcoming me to the whippet family, every one of them eager to tell me what I ought to be doing next. There was a nice woman who ran the RSPCA kennels and another lady, called Judith, who'd come over from Newport. There was also a fella called

Paul who had a butcher's shop in Blaenavon and his wife Joan, who were particularly helpful.

'Number one,' Paul said, 'you should join the Whippet Club of Wales. I'm on the committee, so if you have any problems you give me a ring.'

'That's lovely, that is, thank you.'

'As for more practical things, your best bet is to go to training classes, get the puppy really standing well. She looks nice, she looks like she has potential' – everyone said that to be fair – 'but you need to get her obedient and poised.'

I joined the club immediately – 1983 it was – and poured over all the bumf they sent me on showing whippets and rearing them and breeding them. I was in my element. I felt like a military general planning his tactics for the next attack.

I got Lady down to the training school. It was a mix of obedience basics plus what you needed for showing and competitions: how to walk, how to run, how to stand – we really put her through her paces. You wouldn't think there's a right and a wrong way of standing still but the list of dos and don'ts would amaze you. Lady was a quick learner and I wasn't too bad either so as her birthday approached I began looking around for a competition. Just to dip our toe in the water. By chance the first one open to all-comers was back at Tredegar so that's where I filled in the forms and waited for the invite.

I was itching to get going but luckily another little event cropped up. At the end of the term, the training school had a little competition. It was just sprung upon us after one of the lessons. Well, I loved that. Lady was a star, I was in my element showing off, and lo and behold we only went and won first prize. Brian had driven us up there so he was the only audience but that didn't matter. We had an old convertible at the time so on the way home we put down the roof and I stood up waving our trophy for all the other drivers to see.

Silly but you gotta do it.

When we received the programme for Tredegar I was doing cartwheels seeing my name and Lady's in black and white. I couldn't wait to get there.

When the big day came, obviously I was only there for the experience – I said that to anyone who would listen – but you know how adrenaline gets you, especially when you have a little gold-coloured egg cup from your previous competition sitting on the shelf at home. I looked round at the 'opposition' – for the next couple of hours that's what they were! – and I felt my adrenaline get up.

There's no one here better than my girl.

That was confirmed to me when I saw a woman with a dog of similar colours to mine.

'Oh, they look like twins,' I said. 'They're both brown and white.'

'I don't know what yours is but mine is brindle parti.'

I looked it up later. It means 'brown and white'.

They don't teach you about people like that at training classes. But that wasn't the only thing that caught me out. I must have been away the day the trainer taught us that it's not just the dog on show. It's you.

I'm not as reticent as my husband, far from it, but I didn't quite expect to be under so much scrutiny myself. Being larger than life at the training centre was one thing – I knew everyone there. Here, I wouldn't have said I was among friends, let's put it that way, and the pressure builds as a result.

In the first round, you have to walk the dog in a circle with everyone else. That's fine, I suppose, there's plenty of other faces to look at, but I couldn't help feeling there were a lot of eyes on me. As a newbie you doubt everything you do. The second round is even more daunting because it's one on one. Whippets are judged on tables and you have to stand there while this stranger goes all over them to make sure their mouth is correct, their tail doesn't rise higher than their back, their ears don't point and they are standing straight with the head at the perfect angle. I was nervous and I wasn't even the one doing it.

Poor Lady, I thought, but she seemed to cope okay. At the end they watched her walk again with everyone else and one by one the dogs they liked were removed from the ring. After the first three had gone I was ready to go home. That was it, my dream was over.

I didn't realize the awards went lower than third.

When I got the tap on my shoulder for fourth place I could have screamed. By the time the presentation ceremony took place a while later it still hadn't sunk in. We'd done it. We'd taken a dog, found it a good partner and made something special the other end. And we'd done it from scratch. We got a little award with her show name 'Davokes Romantic Notions' proudly engraved.

A lot of our new friends were there. One or two weren't quite as friendly, if I'm honest, now we'd beaten their dogs, but overall there was genuine pleasure for us.

'You've done something special there,' Paul said. 'Most of the people who beat you here bought their dogs in, they didn't rear them themselves.'

'Where's the fun in that? You may as well cheat on your exam paper.'

He laughed.

I couldn't understand that myself. I mean, I knew it went on. That's how my father had made his money with the budgies, breeding them for other people to enter into competitions. I suppose you can get into a discussion about nature and nurture but if you've got two ugly hounds mating don't be surprised if your puppies have faces only a mother could love. Of course luck plays a part but you can't do much about that, can you? What I was left with was science and probability so those are the factors I decided to concentrate on.

*

A lot of the other competitors pampered their dogs when they weren't showing. I was reminded of Mrs Jones and that horrible poodle that used to live opposite us. I don't think I ever saw it get a single paw muddy.

Lady wasn't so fortunate. Or maybe she was more so. That's how I prefer to see it. That weekend Brian and I went out coursing and of course we took our award-winner with us.

As Brian said, 'What's the point of having a whippet and running yourself?'

We had some fun with that dog. She took us all over, showing, and, you'd better believe it, winning as well. Then came the big one. We were a bit disappointed with just third place in the Limit Bitch category at the Driffield Agricultural Championship Show but it came with an added bonus: qualification to a certain competition run by the Kennel Club down in London. We knew it was a possibility but seeing it written there in black and white was something else.

'Brian,' I said, my hand quivering as I held the letter, 'we're going to Crufts.'

The world's largest and most prestigious dog show, and little old me and my pooch had been invited. How was that for a young woman from the Valleys with no breeding experience? I wish I could say it was a dream ending, but one minute inside that giant aircraft hangar they call Earls Court and I had a bad feeling. The event was so vast and I felt lost if I'm honest and perhaps a little bit out of my depth. Not because I didn't trust my dog, far from it. It was the other owners. Everyone seemed to know the right people. I only knew my husband and my dog. When the early rounds were over I swear the dogs who went through had the most popular owners. And by 'popular', I mean they had owners who'd been laughing and pally with the judges earlier.

I was so mad. I nearly gave it up there and then but of course stubbornness is a quality I was born with and, if anything, I've developed it. It's virtually my superpower. Suffice to say we entered every single competition I could find after that, all over the country. And you know what? With my new insight into the industry I picked the winners every other time. Not because of the dogs, sadly. I'd just have a quick scan down the list of entrants, look at who the judges were and I'd predict the result. It's common sense, really. If you're showing a dog and you know you'll be judging that judge's dog at the next event you've got a very, very good chance of some silverware, haven't you? Talk about scratch my back and I'll scratch yours. I hated it. I hated being part of it but I just could not give up.

Lady did us proud and the name Davokes Romantic Notions appeared on many a trophy, but her best result was a beautiful brood of puppies. One of those, Peggy Sue, continued her mother's good work winning trophies all over. She was also the reason we ended up in

Doncaster one weekend, where I finally got the message about the sport.

Frank Moore is a lovely man, and a great breeder and competitor. We got chatting, he admired my dog and at the end of the day he said, 'Let me have Peggy Sue and I will make her up to a champion for you and we'll get a litter of puppies out of her.'

He knew what he was talking about, no doubt about that, but I had to say no.

'I'd love nothing more than for you to be a winner, Frank, but if my dog is going to be a champion she's going to do it with me in charge. I'm not here for the money or the glory. I just want to see how far I can go on my talents.'

'You may as well pack up now then,' a lady we often saw at shows piped up.

'I beg your pardon?' I said.

She looked at me, eye to eye. 'You have to do your apprenticeship. That's how it works.'

'You're telling me I'm not good enough?'

Oh, her face.

'No, no, Janet, far from it! I'm saying how it is. There are people in this room who won't look at your dog twice if you haven't put in what they consider a decent apprenticeship.'

'How long does that take?'

'It took me about ten years. But don't lose heart!'

Oh, the air was blue. I wasn't angry at her. It was the

set-up. I hate privilege for privilege's sake, always. And what really gets my goat is the old boy network. Look after your own and all that crap doesn't wash with me. Get there on merit or not at all. How can you look yourself in the mirror otherwise? That was the last straw.

I said, 'Are you telling me that even though I have a beautiful dog, because I haven't been showing for long enough I will never get her to the top?'

She shrugged. 'It's not personal. I just don't want you blaming yourself when things don't go as you hope.'

Part of me wished she was just being spiteful because that would mean there was a chance she was wrong. But actually she was a lovely lady, she was just being straight. In fact Lady, Peggy Sue and another dog I bred, Charlie, all won plenty of prizes to prove otherwise. But every so often you'd get a result that just seemed plain wrong.

I remember one event in particular. It was a boiling hot day and in that weather the worst place you can be is under canvas. I was half tempted to turn around again when I saw the tent. I said to Brian, 'It's not fair Peggy Sue having to be out in this heat.'

He said, 'Well, stuck in the car for another three hours going home isn't going to improve anything. You may as well make the best of it.'

We had a few hours till the first round so I put Peggy Sue in her crate in a tent and covered the thing with wet towels to keep her as cool as possible. I thought it might even help her hydration. Common sense, right?

Anyone who knows anything about animals would have done the same. But I didn't see any other dogs in there.

Funny, I thought. *Maybe they're all in the shade elsewhere.*

I was on the verge of thinking we'd done something wrong when we stepped into the show tent and there were most of the other competitors – with their desiccated doggies slumped against them. I couldn't believe it. It must have been more than ninety degrees in there. Those animals were wilting on their feet. But at least the owners could be sure no competitors were tampering with their prize possessions.

'These people don't deserve animals,' Brian said. 'How are they going to win anything with a dog that can't even stand up?'

The show started and Peggy Sue was alert as any creature could be in those conditions. She sailed through the walking, the examination on the mat and the group presentation. All around her there were poodles and greyhounds and bulldogs half asleep on their leads. One was so lethargic he had to be half carried around the ring.

But that didn't stop him winning.

Honestly, if I had any doubts about the sport they were confirmed that day. So many people came up to me afterwards to say I should have won. There were strangers and even one or two people who wouldn't normally count me as a friend, but they all said the same thing: 'You know the winner's judging the next week, don't you?'

'Yeah,' I said. 'I hope their car breaks down on the way home.'

'I can make sure of it if you want,' Brian said.

He was joking but my God it was tempting.

What made us different from some owners was that winning wasn't the be-all and end-all for us. Peggy Sue's comfort came at the top of the list. That's why we liked to keep up the coursing with the dogs. She came out just like her mother and I think it really helped us to see them let their hair down. It was exactly the same with Davokes Rags To Riches – or 'Charlie' as we called him. He was another amazing winner. It was Brian as usual who selected him from the new litter as the one that was going to pull up trees and I quickly saw he was right. If anything, I fast-tracked that dog. I worked it out that there was a competition taking place in London on the exact day he was six months old.

'Come on, Charlie boy,' I said, 'we're off to the Smoke.'

I hate going to London usually but this felt too good an opportunity to pass up. It seemed to be fate, almost, that this show was on the first day he could legally participate. Either way, we went, we saw, we conquered.

And I got another invite to Crufts. In his first competition! Everyone was so happy for us but then I dropped the bombshell.

'We won't be going.'

'Why ever not?'

'Where do I start? The old boys' network, the travel, the hanging around, the whole city being up itself? No, I'm happy knowing we were good enough. I don't want to go there and feel cheated again.'

Friends, strangers, all sorts, they all tried to persuade me that Crufts was an honour they'd kill for. But I had my superpower and there was no changing my mind, not even when he won another Crufts entry in Manchester the following year. I'm only interested in competitions I can win. Like I said, science and probability, those are my skills. With Crufts as it was back then, I felt that all the science in the canine world wouldn't help me beat a hundred people who'd done their decade's apprenticeship. That's where the probability came in.

Of course, chance plays its part as well. You might say I should have foreseen the dangers of letting our dogs come coursing with us but they're not clockwork. You can't wrap them in cotton wool. Occasionally accidents do happen and there's nothing you can do.

We were out working one weekend as usual, down in Bedwellty round the corner. Susie was doing her job in the hedge, sniffing out the rabbit. Bingo, she gets the scent and the bunny comes shooting out. That's enough for Charlie, he's off like a rocket. Just as he reaches the rabbit, the spaniel comes haring out of the undergrowth and they collide. Travelling at that speed with no fat on you is going to hurt and poor Charlie went over and over. He was whimpering and crying. The vet said he'd put his shoulder out and it would heal enough to run again.

'What about showing?'

He shook his head. 'I'm no judge,' he said, 'but if this shoulder is half an inch lower than the other the experts are going to notice.'

I was so sad for that dog. Charlie was a natural poser, a beautiful boy and, who knows, if we were still winning Crufts invites after ten years maybe I would have bitten the bullet and let him have his day in the sun. As it was, Davokes Rags To Riches retired that day with full honours.

Not to be mean, but I wish I could say that this disappointment reverberated further than the four walls of our own house. Charlie deserved as much attention as possible but the truth is, people in Cefn Fforest and all areas around Wales had bigger worries on their minds. Even the people in my own family. After all, what was the future of one dog when an entire region's livelihood was at stake?

It was 1984 and Arthur Scargill had just called a strike.

4

They'd Need Engines

When something is all around you all the time it's somehow easier to forget. Like the air you breathe or maybe even the neighbours you wave to every day. You take them for granted and just assume they'll always be there.

It was the same with the coal.

I hadn't really thought about the black stuff, if I'm honest, since I worked at the National Coal Board. Even then I was in ancillary services, office-based stuff, so I wasn't exactly at the coal face. The last time it had made a conscious impression on me was when I was a child. Seeing your dad come home covered in coal dust every night was something you couldn't forget. Mainly, though, it was playing in the slag heaps that I really recalled. Even as an adult I couldn't bring myself to think the tips were eyesores. They were as much a part of the landscape as the green hills and the plunging valleys.

The truth is, our entire region was totally dependent on the coal. Young girls working in the head office in

Cardiff like I did, they wouldn't be there without the coal. The miners, obviously, they needed the coal, but then so did their families, their children and any parents they were looking after. Coal money paid for their lunch, their Christmas presents, their toothpaste even. The local shops, the local businesses, they could trace the majority of their takings back to coal money. Take Brian: he was on the lorries and, while it was a private company, the majority of their business was shipping coal from here to there. Most of his brothers worked in the pits. The one that didn't was an electrician – *for the coal board*. There were doctors, plumbers, builders, all sorts who, on paper, had universally applicable jobs but, when you looked at them, totally depended on the mines for their customers and their income. With the strike it was all gone.

It affected everyone. Even in his fifties my dad was working down there with my brother, who still lived at home, so when the pair of them joined the walkout it left my mum's factory wage supporting the three of them.

It was hard sometimes to know which way to think. The miners were striking for improved conditions, better hours, better pay. If it came off, the short-term pain would provide long-term gain. That was the miners' union's logic. Those of us on the outside looking in weren't going to benefit directly from those improvements, but we were all suffering. Brian drove for a private firm. If the strikers got their new deal that wouldn't affect his company one bit. Bearing in mind he could sometimes pick up coal from one colliery and the next day there'd be nothing because of the strike, he was suffering without any promise of improvements further down the line. If I'm honest, the longer it went on the more it created a bit of discontent locally. There were people who said that, since the entire region depended on the coal, the miners had a duty to return to work. If they didn't they were in danger of destroying the area. Of course, they said that if they didn't protect the industry the government would kill it off anyway.

All we knew for sure was that when the pits shut down, everybody suffered. And I mean *everybody*.

There was a load of anger in the area of course. Most of it was directed at Margaret Thatcher's policy towards the industry. As far as we could tell, the prime minister and her Tory government wanted to shut down the mines at any cost. If they could destroy the trade union movement in the process that would be a bonus. A big bonus.

It's a long while ago now but the leader of the National Union of Mineworkers, Arthur Scargill, like Neil Kinnock around the same time, got a raw deal in the media, I felt. I'd seen enough suspect scoring with the whippets to recognize a newspaper story that wasn't telling the truth in case it offended its owner's Conservative friends. But that didn't mean the man was a saint. There was a lot of controversy over the way Scargill ran his union and especially about how he conducted the strike. The biggest problem – his biggest mistake it's said – was not having a national ballot. Unions back then had a lot of legislative power if they played by the rules. The 1970s were littered with very successful legal strike action. By calling for a national strike without a proper vote Scargill opened himself up for some heavy-handed tactics from Mrs Thatcher and the police. And we all know how it ended.

When it started, mind, no one could see what was around the corner. All we knew was that the collieries weren't producing anything. The miners were standing guard outside and no one was going in or out. Which meant no one was being paid.

It's fair to say it broke us. Broke us all. It was the death of the community. There was nothing else here. No plan B. When the strike ended in failure and the government finally got its way and shut the majority of the industry down there was no safety net. People were out of work and felt disenfranchised from their country, to be honest. For more than a year we felt like we were at war with the government. Parliament wasn't our church and those in Whitehall weren't our friends. The suits in Westminster wanted to destroy us, it was plain as day. Of course they weren't going to look after us when the dispute ended.

Years later and you see these men who were young at the time wandering around. A lot of them never bothered at school because they knew they had a job for life in the soot. When it was taken away it was like they'd lost a limb or, worse, their marbles. When you lose your spirit your body follows, and vice versa. I've seen some sorry sights. Men who still haven't recovered today from being thrown on the scrapheap in the prime of their years. They're a generation younger than me and they look older.

We all suffered, of course. Brian's job went the way of the mines. No coal, no lorry drivers required. Luckily, he picked up a position soon enough with the local council doing the roads – tarmacking, repairing, building, that sort of thing. Brian being Brian he loved it. It was a bit hard going, as he was beginning to feel pain in his joints, but he loved the challenge of keeping up with the younger men on his crew.

Thirty years later – a generation you could say – nothing has improved. Traditional labour has all but vanished. Shops are boarded up and there are very few factories. Over at Oakdale they make batteries and carpets, but everything else has gone. Even the sewing factory's days were numbered back then. We just didn't know it. In recent years the biggest new employer has been the new Asda superstore. Basically if you want a job now you have to get over to Cardiff.

So much for never having to leave the Valleys. Living and dying in God's own country. These days if you don't leave then dying isn't a possibility. It's a certainty.

One way or another time catches us all up. Especially if bad luck is helping it out. After nine very, very good years breeding the whippets – winning entry to Crufts virtually every year up to 1991 – we decided to knock it on the head. To get the best out of the dogs they needed exercise and Brian was finding it increasingly difficult to get about. It didn't help that his job was so physically demanding.

We put it down to lack of fitness at first, then maybe oncoming old age. The doctors eventually got round to running some X-rays and it turned out his hips were gone. Riddled with arthritis. Suddenly everything changed. Brian was put on the list for a double hip replacement and as a result had no choice but to retire on the sick from the council.

We sold the young dogs. It's heartbreaking saying goodbye to pups you've bred and reared yourself, and even harder when they've done you proud at championships. Two of ours, King Of The Road and Pinball Wizard, were both very successful and therefore quite valuable. We hung on to the older ones, Peggy, Lady and Charlie – not to show, just to live out their days in comfort. They'd paid their dues, it was only right we looked after them now.

One of the reasons I think I was successful with the dogs was I wasn't that bothered. Don't get me wrong, I wanted to win, but only on my terms. What was more important to me was having some respect at the end of it, that's why I always bred my own show dogs. I don't want some flatpack poodle, I want to build my own from scratch.

I also wanted to spend quality time with my husband. Thanks to those dogs we'd be up and down the motorways every weekend, sometimes twice, going anywhere from Cornwall to Scotland and, occasionally, if we were lucky, waving a trophy out the roof. For those two reasons I wasn't overly worried about prizes and prize money. Beating more expensive dogs was a lottery win for me. Which was just as well because one day I decided to tot up what I'd spent. Charlie had been the most successful so I went through my bank statements and had a look at what I'd coughed up.

Quite a lot it turned out.

If I tell you I stopped counting at £3,000 over eighteen months you'll have some idea. I was still showing at the time and I thought, *Oh my God, if I keep adding up it will make me stop with the dogs.* And I didn't want that. I didn't begrudge Charlie the money but it did make me think of my five-and-a-half-day a week shift at the sewing factory in a different light. I was basically working day and night to keep my show dog in glitter.

Maybe I needed to find a cheaper hobby?

As one door closes another one opens. Never has a truer sentence been said. In our instance, though, that door had been open a long while and we'd never noticed. It was another case of something being around so much you don't think about it. It wasn't the air that we breathe or the neighbours we acknowledge, it was birds. Pigeons to be precise.

We were over at one of Brian's brothers. Kenny his name is. It was a beautiful hot summer's evening so we were sitting in the garden enjoying a cold drink. For me and Brian that was enough. After a hard day's work the pair of us just wanted to close our eyes and let the warmth wash over us. For Kenny, it wasn't a time to relax. Not yet. His eyes were fixed on the sky. He wasn't watching the sun, mind. He was waiting for his birds to come home.

I was basking in the evening rays when I heard Kenny get excited. He started cooing like a bird and waving his arms. Squinting into the light I saw a little grey missile land on the roof of the outbuilding down the garden. Then, two hops and it was inside. Kenny followed it in then emerged a few minutes later.

'That's her caged, clocked and fed,' he said. 'Just one more to come now.'

Most of Brian's family raced pigeons. His dad had always had them and Kenny and the rest just carried it on when they got their own places. On this particular day Kenny was competing in the Welsh National, the biggest event around. The birds had been released from miles away – hundreds of miles probably – and they had to find their way home. Each pigeon had a little ring on its leg with a unique number. They were 'clocked', as they called it, on take off and clocked again by the owners when they landed. Once everyone's birds had returned the organizers would examine the clock times and announce a winner.

It all sounded rather exciting. More than that, though, imagine having a bird coming when you called it. They can go anywhere in the sky yet they choose to return to you. I thought that was lovely. And the look on Kenny's face when he saw them on the horizon was a picture. The more I saw the more I thought, *I could have a bit of fun with these.*

'Brian,' I said, 'I wouldn't mind having a bird or two in the garden.'

He nearly spat his drink out. 'Oh, give over,' he spurted. 'I had enough of those rats with wings when I was growing up. I'm sick of them.'

Kenny was straight over.

'Oh, leave it alone, Daisy, not everyone is scared of little birds.'

'I'm not scared of anything,' Brian said.

'What's the problem then? If Jan wants a couple of pigeons let her have a couple of pigeons. Where's the harm?'

Brian had his face in his hands by now.

'Have you met my wife?' he groaned. 'It won't just be a couple with her, will it?'

'Give over,' I said. 'What do you think I'm going to do with them?'

'Honestly,' he said, 'I don't know. But I bet it will mean work enough for me.'

Kenny clapped his hands. 'That's decided then,' he said. 'I'll start you off with three pairs, Janet, and if you take to them you can always get some more.'

Poor Brian. If he shook his head any more I swear it would have unscrewed from his neck.

'Come on, you miserable bugger,' Kenny said. 'Where's the harm in a few birds?'

'Ask me that again in six months.'

Brian wasn't totally wrong. I mean, the birds needed somewhere to live, didn't they? I made a few noises about doing it myself but obviously when it came to converting our shed into a pigeon loft Brian ended up doing the work. He put a little trap in it, just like his dad and brothers had, so the birds could get in easily enough. Once we were all set, we let our birds have a week or so in their new home then took them out for a drive. We couldn't go too far in case of traffic. All I wanted was to see them flying home. If we went an excessive distance they'd be home before us.

Sometimes I think I know my husband better than he knows himself. It's possible it also works the other way round. I had no intention of racing those birds when I decided to get them. The thrill of waiting for them to come home was all I wanted out of it. For months I was happy with the status quo and then one day I thought,

Well, I've got them now, haven't I? And they certainly know their way home. Maybe I'm being cruel not racing them?

Brian didn't know whether to laugh or cry. 'I knew it, I knew it,' he said. 'You're so competitive. I knew you'd bloody want to go racing.'

I looked into it and to race you need to belong to a club because you need somewhere to go to ring the birds, keep the records and organize everything. Where we lived in Cfen Fforest, there wasn't a club; you had to go to Bargoed or Pontypridd. That sounded like something that could be improved. Just by talking to people I knew I wasn't the only one with birds so I said to Brian, 'Why don't we start our own club? There are enough pigeon fanciers around here to get it going.'

Obviously he didn't want to approach strangers, but we compromised and sent out letters to all the pigeon fanciers we were aware of in the village. People were generally positive and a few months later we got going officially. We used the local institute as our base of operations and over a weekend everyone brought their birds to be registered. You put a numbered ring on the bird's leg, like Kenny had done, then we recorded them in a book. Everybody had a clock to monitor their birds' times. When your pigeon came home you took the rubber ring off, put it on a thimble, put it in the clock and the time got stamped on the ring. It's a funny way to race because unless one person owns all the birds they each have different destinations and distances to fly. Time is only one of the factors we looked at though. Velocity and distance were key as well. You might have a pigeon coming first but someone living a bit further away, even if their birds come in after yours, might have flown quicker. And that's what we're interested in. Every loft is marked on a map so when you say your bird did such-a-such time we can see how far he had to go and work out an average speed.

It makes it a bit thrilling because you don't know who's won until you hand your clock in and compare it against the others.

The best bit about racing pigeons, though, is the effort. With Brian struggling with stiff joints, it was lovely to have a hobby that didn't require us to do much more than register the birds. If you entered a competition, a lorry would drive around the area and pick up your crate of entrants and take them all to the race point. Usually that takes about a day, so the next morning they're all released and all you have to do is sit in your garden and monitor the sky.

For all his moaning, Brian decided to get involved as well so he built his own loft further down the garden. It's funny sharing your hobby with your husband when he's also your main competitor. To think he could have been doing it decades earlier with his dad.

Speaking of my father-in-law, he'd long since passed but in his honour I'd called my fastest bird Will's Dream

– him being called William Vokes. At least, I think it was my fastest. Whippets can look quite similar but pigeons are damn impossible to tell apart. When Brian was taking the birds out further each time I noticed that a certain one was heading the pack on the return. There was something about the way it flew that made it stand out against the others. By the time it landed though, and disappeared inside the loft, it was like finding a needle in a haystack.

It didn't really matter. When our first race came round I boxed them all up. Brian did the same with his. They were collected and the next day we waited on tenter-hooks. Sure enough, I recognized my first bird's flying gait so I made a note of the number and against it wrote 'Will's Dream'. Whether his Dad was looking down on me or not I don't know, but his namesake won that race. First the whippets and now the pigeons. What's not to like about coming first?

As usual I had a feeling that I could be doing more. The good few wins that Brian and I shared over the next few years came on what was called the 'North Road' course – basically, the birds were released in North Wales, Northern England or Scotland. That was okay but in all the reading I was doing on the subject – and of course I was devouring every book or magazine I could find – the 'South Road' seemed the place to compete. Birds on that course were launched from as far afield as the Isle of Wight, France or even Belgium. It was so exotic and so, so dangerous. The birds had to fly over vast expanses of water. If they got tired, unless they could find a ferry to land on, they'd have to keep going.

I wasn't the one flying but I fancied a few of my birds in particular to be stayers. The South Road, I realized, was where I needed to be.

Brian was on a bit of a winning streak with the North Road so when I asked him to switch codes he declined. Everyone from my pigeon club said the same: 'It's too dangerous.'

'Where's your ambition?'

'Where's your common sense?'

Fair point. I was about to give up when I got a phone call from a fella. He said, 'Hello, my name's Des Powell. I've got a bird with your phone number on its ankle.'

'Oh, thank the lord,' I said. 'One of them didn't come home yesterday. I thought he'd been got by buzzards.'

'No, no, he's in one piece, just a bit lost I'd say.'

'Where are you then?' I asked.

He said, 'Caldicot.'

'Well, I suppose we had better come and get him.'

The next day Brian and I drove over there. The bird in question wasn't one of my racers. I just let him out every day and he flew around and came back in his own time. Maybe he had more potential than I thought.

Des was an elderly gentleman who lived on his own. He was lovely. He took us in and he showed us his garden and we saw his trophies where he had won a few nationals with his birds. We got chatting and I said how

I wanted to fly in the South Road but everyone kept advising me against it, and he said, 'Don't listen to anyone. If you want to fly in the South, my girl, you fly in the South. If you can't find a club to support you then join the nationals.'

Looking at all his trophies I thought, *This is a man who knows what he's talking about.* So I joined the South Wales National. My first race was due to be from Ventnor on the Isle of Wight. I didn't want to leave anything to chance so, to practise, I sent Brian over the bridge into Newport to release my birds from there. If they wanted to get home they'd have to fly over the water. I used to finish work at the sewing factory at five so if he released them then we'd all get home together. We did that every day for a week. Will's Dream was first back every time.

I wondered what else I could do to prepare. In an old book I found a recipe of honey and pinhead oats – basically oat kernels that have been chopped into two or three pieces. It's so fine it's meant to be easier for the birds to digest. I thought, *That makes sense*, so I got chopping and mixing and two nights before the race I fed my birds the new concoction.

The next day I had to get them clocked. Our nearest marking station for the nationals was in Nelson, a village about five miles north of Caerphilly and another five north of Cardiff. It was a Friday, so after work we put a dozen birds in the crate and off we went. I put the box down by the clocking desk and waited in the queue. When we opened it up I couldn't believe it. All twelve birds were lying on the floor.

Oh crap, what have I done?

Everyone who saw them burst out laughing. All their birds were alert and twitching like they were on sentry duty.

'What's wrong with your birds, Janet?' someone said. 'Having a kip are they?'

I wanted the ground to open up. The only person not smiling was the young lad doing the clocks.

'Do you still want to enter them?' he asked, all earnest.

'What do you think?'

'Well, you've come this far. You wouldn't have brought them if they were ill.'

'You're right,' I said. 'Ring 'em up.'

By the time we got the birds home they were a bit perkier. I fed them my special recipe and was shocked to see them go all sleepy again. I was so worried. What if I was sending them to their death? Pigeons can't swim, not in the sea anyway. Had I poisoned them, was that it? When the lorry came for pickup I nearly didn't let them go. Brian had to say, 'They'll be fine, trust yourself.'

'You're right,' I said, 'I've done the best I can.'

I'm not particularly religious, if I'm honest, but nodding off that night I thought, *If there's anyone listening, please bring my birds home safe and dry and sound.*

I didn't expect a reply – and certainly not from the person who popped up.

I was sound asleep and I heard this voice.

'Don't worry about your birds.'

I opened my eyes – or so I thought – and standing in front of me was Brian's father, William, long since passed away. Now, logic tells me it was a dream but at that moment he was as real to me as anyone I'd seen that day.

'Janet,' he said, 'you've nothing to fear. Your birds will find their way but that's not all. You're going to win the National.'

'Win it?' I said.

He nodded.

'How do you know?'

'I just do.'

He smiled and I did the same. Then I forgot all about it.

At eleven o'clock the next morning, three hours into my half-day shift at the factory, I suddenly sat bolt upright.

'I'm going to win,' I said.

'What's that, Jan?' the woman nearest me said.

'Oh nothing.' I smiled. 'Just remembering an old friend.'

I got home after work and Brian said, 'The birds are in the air. We've probably got another hour.'

From Ventnor to ours was 115 miles. I didn't envy any

of them. At least they'd have some properly digested food.

I made a cup of tea, got the garden chairs out and settled down with a book. About thirty minutes later something caught the corner of my eye and made me look up. Three tiny specks in the distance were heading our way.

'Oh my God, they're coming,' I said.

Brian laughed. 'It's too early. They'd need engines to do it in that time.'

I wasn't having it. 'I know my birds. And I definitely know that one at the front.'

I'd recognize Will's Dream's wing pattern any day. After all those times scrutinizing him it was etched on my brain. Brian stayed in his chair for a while and only when they got closer, when you could see their colouring, did he leap up.

'Christ, you're right.'

He was like a man possessed after that. Whooping and cooing and waving and dancing. He was doing everything to entice those birds down. I don't know if it helped but they swooped down and we clicked them all against the clock.

'I don't believe that,' he said.

'Neither do I. But the proof is in the pudding. We'll find out tomorrow how we did.'

Our trip to Nelson on Sunday was lovely. When the race is over people are friendlier. A fellow fancier from our village, also called Brian, came with us. He only flew in the North Road but he wanted to see how the nationals worked.

Was he in for a treat.

With the dogs, the snobbery and the old boy's network really took the edge off my time showing the whippets. In pigeons, I'd never met anyone saying 'you need to serve an apprenticeship' or anything like that. But then I'd never done the nationals before. We got to the tent to get the clock marked and suddenly I saw a whole new side of the sport.

The fellow opening my clock to get the official knock time was meant to be impartial. 'Meant to be' being the operative words. I think he must have had a few bob on another bird because he saw my times and said, 'This can't be right.'

'What's the problem?' I asked.

'Your clock wasn't knocked properly,' he said. 'There's no way those half-dead birds of yours I saw on Friday could do these times.'

I was lost for words. Luckily our friend Brian wasn't. He kicked up a right fuss at top volume.

'You have no right to accuse these people of anything,' he shouted. 'You set the clocks, you abide by their times. It's not rocket science.'

Before the steward could answer, the young lad who'd originally seen to us on Friday came running in. 'What's all the noise?' he asked.

'This man is saying we've cheated because of our clock times.'

He looked at me, picked up the clock then looked directly at the steward. 'There is nothing wrong with this clock. I knocked it myself. You need to apologize.'

Bless him, he didn't need to go out on a limb like that. Not at his age.

But that wasn't the end of it. The bolshie steward wasn't alone in his questioning of my abilities as a novice competitor. A bloke about two down in the queue snatched the paper with my times on it and announced, 'Don't worry about her dodgy clock, my birds have won enough nationals to have beaten these amateurs' times easily.'

If Brian hadn't been on two sticks from his hip replacements I think that fella would have discovered how much my husband doesn't care for bullies. As it was, the bloke was lucky not to get a whack around the head. Brian was seething. Other Brian wasn't far behind.

'It's only pigeon flying for goodness' sake!' I said. 'It's not horse racing.'

Because the other bloke made such a fuss the people behind us in the line let him jump the queue. When his clock printout was handed over I didn't snatch it off him. I didn't need to. I could tell everything from his face.

He went to say something, then looking at both Brians' faces he thought better of it. He stuck his nose in the air, turned and marched out of the tent.

*

And that is the story of how Will's Dream won a National – and I couldn't have done it without his namesake, my father-in-law. To this day I can't be sure he wasn't actually standing there. Sometimes, I think, things are just meant to be.

There was prize money for coming first. Not enough to retire on, but it paid for a tidy meal. Funnily enough, although Will's Dream came first in a dozen or more big races, we won much more money on some of his loft mates who never got higher than third. When you enter a bird into a race you pay an entry fee. Back then, you could pay two pounds, a quid or 50p. But then you can bet on your bird for the race. To scoop the jackpot your pigeon doesn't have to win the event, it just needs to be the first of its price category to come home. So yes, Will's Dream got us all the headlines – and several lovely commemorative plates from the nationals – but lesser flyers won us the cash. I had one that never saw first place in a race in the North Road in his life but he was more often than not the first of his category home. I'm not kidding you, that bird paid for Brian and me to have a decent holiday in Egypt to celebrate our twenty-fifth wedding anniversary. Up until then the pigeons had travelled more than I had. Two grand that holiday cost. I don't think Will's Dream would have paid for more than a flight.

Of course, I never competed for money. I don't see the point. There are better ways to get rich. All I wanted, all I've ever wanted, was to prove that I can do whatever I set my mind to. If it's against the odds, fabulous. And if it means going up against a bunch of old fogeys in flat caps who tell me I don't know what I'm doing, even better.

He wasn't a fogey, but I adored racing against my husband. I think he'd admit I had the upper hand most days but if anyone ever came around the garden to look at the birds you'd never guess. After I won the National our visitors increased tenfold. They wanted to know the secrets of my success. Where do they sleep? What do you feed them? What's the training? They all had their notebooks out.

If I was busy Brian would take guests round the lofts. I came home earlier than expected once and caught the tour. In his loft he said, 'I won so-and-so national with this, I won this with this, I won that with that,' then he went into my loft and said, '*We* won this with that, *we* won the National with that.' God love him. His birds were his birds but I had to share my victories. That's marriage for you . . .

As I say, he'd admit I had the better run. One day he was miserable because his birds just weren't good enough. He didn't have a single rat with wings that could compete. The South Road season had just finished so he asked if I would lend him a few flyers for his race up north. Obviously I said yes. He got them ready, crated them up and put them on the lorry.

Later that night we heard the news. The lorry had had

a fire. All the birds were gone. The ones that weren't killed took off and never came home. Can't blame them really.

We had to start from scratch after that. We both got back into the scene and had some wins with our new birds but it wasn't the same. They're not the same as dogs but no one likes to think of their birds hurting. My next batch were perfectly fine but the buzz had gone.

It didn't help that I decided to take on another job. I wish I could say that I was living up to my promise to myself and going back into office work but I wasn't. A working men's club round the way from our house was advertising for a weekend barmaid so I decided to apply. They said yes and I started straight away. My new hours took up a lot of the weekend, which was prime flying time, so I knocked the racing on the head. I gave the birds to an old boy in Wrexham who'd lost everything in the lorry fire and I gave the clock to a lad in the village who was just starting out as a fancier.

The sewing factory was still good for me stability-wise, although every day I punched in was a reminder I could – and *should* – have been doing something more worthwhile with my education. But by then the Coal Board was virtually non-existent, so you could say I'd dodged a bullet by getting out early. Perhaps fifteen years early is a tad extreme but better premature than late. Luck, as I say, has a hand in everything. The timing of one thing impacts the next. For example, if we hadn't given up the dogs when we did I'd have never got into the pigeons. And if we didn't give up the pigeons I would never have been in the working men's club to overhear the conversation that was about to change my life.

5

Bloomin' Horses

What began as a few weekend shifts at the Top Club pulling pints extended to running the place. Never one to turn down a challenge, obviously I was quick to agree to become manager. Most of my responsibilities were confined to the organization of the venue, sorting out bookings, contracting cleaners and suppliers, things like that. During busy periods, though, I put aside my clipboard and rolled up my sleeves. It was one such night in 1998, we had some old time dancing going on in the concert hall and I was helping on the drinks.

As a barmaid you're either the most important person in the room – if someone's trying to get a drink that is – or little more than a fly on the wall if they've already been served. It's amazing the things people say in front of you. It's like being the Invisible Man.

There were a couple of fellas who came in that night and I knew them both by sight, although neither of them by name. I pulled their pints then went about my other duties while they stayed leaning against the bar. When I came back down their end I couldn't help overhearing what they were chatting about.

Bloomin' horses.

Obviously it's none of my business so I tried to tune out. But soon enough I realized they were talking about something a bit different to the kind of creature Brian rode. One of them was telling his mate about a racehorse he'd once owned with a group of friends.

'It's not that expensive,' he was saying, 'not if you have people contributing.'

'Like a syndicate?' his pal said.

'Exactly. We had everyone paying a fixed amount and that covered the costs. If you get your sums right it's affordable for everyone.'

I was intrigued but there was a sting in the tail. For whatever reason the man's syndicate had gone belly up and they were left with more bills than the weekly subscriptions could cover. When he went to his contributors to settle the debt, they were all suddenly a bit deaf. Short story: he ended up seriously out of pocket.

He was explaining all this to his mate by way of a cautionary tale: 'Don't do this unless you want that', 'Nothing good comes of working in a group', 'You only need money involved to find out who your true friends are'.

Honestly, listening to this voice of doom was like watching a *Panorama* exposé. I'll admit, my interest was piqued. After having my own ups and downs with dogs and pigeons I could empathize. The difference was I came out of both sports smiling. This fella had nothing but bad news about horse racing. He'd been burned financially and learned his lesson.

When they left I asked another customer I'd seen talking to them who the two 'horse' men were.

'I wasn't watching but the one most probably doing all the talking was Howard Davies,' he said. 'He's a tax inspector. His mate I only know to nod to.'

'A tax inspector you say? So he knows about money.'

'What do you want to know for?'

'I'm not sure yet,' I replied.

That was the truth. I'm not one to dwell on things. I got into both dogs and pigeons by accident. If something lights my fire I'll pursue it. If it doesn't, there's always something on TV. Anyway, over the next few days that conversation came back to me. I wasn't sure exactly what to make of it in my own mind but when this Howard Davies happened to walk back in the following Saturday while I was on shift, I had a flash of inspiration. When he came to the bar I made sure I served him.

'You're Howard, aren't you?'

He stared at me quizzically. Perhaps I should have picked an easier question.

'I am,' he said eventually. 'And I hear you're Janet. Now, would you like to pour me a pint?'

'Happily,' I replied. But as we waited for the glass to

fill I said, 'I'm thinking of breeding a racehorse.' The words came out like I'd been planning it all my life.

'Oh yeah?' he said.

'Yes, and I'm going to set up a syndicate to pay for it.'

He laughed. Not in a humorous way. 'Good luck with that.'

'Actually, you're the one who'll need the luck,' I said. 'Because I was hoping you'd set it up for me.'

He nearly choked on his ale.

But he didn't walk away. I'm stubborn, I might have mentioned, so I wasn't letting go. Not unless he really, really begged me to. And, if I'm honest, he never did. He made various negative noises but all I took from it was: he'd been in a syndicate before, they'd bought a horse, it had lost money and as secretary of the syndicate he'd ended up paying the debts out of his own pocket, much to his wife Angela's horror.

'I promised her I'd never have anything to do with the horses again,' he said.

'Let me have a word with her,' I replied. 'She'll come round.'

'Oh no, you're not going anywhere near her. I don't want anything to do with this. And you shouldn't either. No good will come of it, I promise you now.'

When I got home that night Brian was still up.

'I'm glad you're awake,' I said. 'You know how you used to pick the show dogs for me?'

'Aye,' he said. 'Never let you down, did I?'

'No, you didn't. And that's why I want you to do it again.'

'You're going back into dogs?'

'God no. I want you to find me a thoroughbred mare.'

'What? A horse?'

'Yes, Brian, a horse.'

'What on earth for?'

'I'm going to breed a champion racer.'

I don't know who was harder to convince, Brian or Howard. To both of them I said, 'I've bred pigeons and I've bred dogs. Why can't I breed racehorses?'

To which they replied, in their ways, 'Horses are different. They cost thousands. A kid in the street can be your opposition with the pigeons. With horses you'll be up against owners who have their own countries!'

I relished the challenge even more after hearing that. I didn't have two coins to rub together. Nothing would give me greater satisfaction than going up against one of the so-called untouchables.

The only difference between the two men's responses was the language. Howard kept his powder dry, as it were. His emotions were completely in check, as you'd expect considering he didn't know me. Brian, on the other hand, wasn't so restrained.

'Listen to yourself, you silly cow. You don't know the first thing about this. You'll make a fool of yourself. Have you seen the people who go racing? All top hats and tails. What'll they think of us?'

'Oh, Brian love, you can't be scared of other people's opinions all your life. I'm going to give this a go and if it works it works and if it doesn't it doesn't. But I'll be nobody's fool, I promise you that.'

He had a think about that.

'Is there nothing I can say to put you off?'

'No,' I said. 'My mind is made up.'

'Okay, then, let's see how we can make this happen.'

In fact, one of Brian's 'project' horses had a role to play. He had bought a Welsh cob from an old couple, Mr and Mrs Hancock, up in Llandudno, who seemed to know a thing or two about breeding so he asked them for advice. They had a think then Mr Hancock said, 'Now you come to mention it I do know someone with a mare for sale. He's a young lad, David, loves his horses. He won't steer you wrong.'

I'd barely had David's number five minutes before I was on the phone. He sounded as nice as promised. He said he had a mare all right but she'd just foaled so wouldn't be going anywhere. He also had an eighteen-month-old gelding. He couldn't afford to run three horses so his plan was to get shot of one of them.

The gelding sounded promising but I didn't want to buy a horse to race. I didn't want the new foal either. I wanted to make my own from scratch like I'd done with the whippets. That's why I needed a mare.

'Can I come and have a look at her?'

'Of course, but she's not for sale until she's finished with the foal.'

His field was a bit off the beaten track, he said, so he gave me details of where to meet the next day. I hoped I got it right. People say I sound Welsh but I'd never heard such a thick accent before. You could cut it with a knife.

The next day we pulled up in the layby where he said he'd meet us and we waited. And we waited. And waited. After sixty minutes tempers were fraying in the summer heat.

'Are you sure you got the right day?' Brian asked.

'I'm sure.'

'Are you sure you got the right time?'

'I'm sure.'

'And this is definitely the right place?'

I wanted to throttle him. We sat in silence for a few more minutes then Brian said, 'Tell me again how you're meant to recognize him.'

'For goodness' sake, he said he'd be here, seven o'clock, in a grey Skoda. It's only eight o'clock. He's just running late, that's all.'

'Grey Skoda you say?'

'Are you deaf?'

'No, but you might be. There's been a boy down there for an hour on a grey *scooter*.'

God, I hate it when he's right.

We went over and sure enough it was him. We followed the scooter down to the stables and I got so excited as we approached. When we went inside I was pinching myself to keep calm.

'Here she is,' David said, 'here's Rewbell.'

Having seen the gelding there was no question he was handsome, but this mare was a beauty. Lovely chestnut coat, healthy eyes and teeth. And seeing her so good with her foal just proved she was the one for me. I was bubbling. For some reason Brian was less enthusiastic.

'She's got some nasty scars on her legs,' he pointed out. 'Barbed wire by the looks of it.'

David nodded. 'She got scared in a lightning storm. You know what they're like.'

'Oh, I do, that.' He was quiet for a bit while he looked the mare up and down.

'So, how much are you asking for her?' he said.

'A thousand pound.'

'A thousand pound? I'm sorry, lad, she's not worth that. Not with those scars. Who knows what else is wrong with her.'

David was indignant. 'There's nothing wrong with her. I checked her myself.'

'Can I just have a word with my husband?' I said. David nodded and stepped outside the stable.

'What are you doing?' I hissed at him. 'This mare is perfect. Look at her foal. She's easily worth £1,000.'

'I agree,' Brian grinned. 'But the lad doesn't know that.'

We found the boy and Brian said, 'Look, I've got £300 in my pocket. I can put it in your hand right now.'

'That's not enough. The asking price is a thousand.'

Brian pulled the cash out. 'Are you sure? It's my final offer.'

The lad shook his head so we turned to walk back to the car. We barely got halfway when the boy called out, 'Okay, she's yours for 300.'

Bless that lad. I wanted to hug him. I said to Brian, 'How much more have you got in your pocket?'

'About fifty quid.'

'Well, give him that as well for his trouble.'

We couldn't remove Rewbell from the foal so I offered to David to take both, rear the baby then return him when he was old enough. I didn't know the first thing about rearing horses but I assumed Brian would. I just couldn't wait to get my hands on my beautiful mare.

The lad thought about it but he said he'd worry if he wasn't looking after the foal himself – the sign of a good man. Instead, he suggested he'd look after Rewbell while she was being a mother and when we came back in three months she'd be ours. That was fair to everyone, particularly the horses, so we shook on it and off we went back to the car.

That feeling of exhilaration we had when Lady won her first little competition at the training ground – well we had it again as we drove home. I was over-the-moon excited.

'I can't believe we're doing this,' I said. 'We're going to have our own racehorse.'

'I know,' he smiled. 'Now we just have to find a way to pay for it.'

6

No Foal, No Fee

I thought we'd had a good deal at £350. It turned out we got Rewbell for considerably less. If you think about it, we paid in the summer but we weren't going to pick her up until September so that's ten weeks of free bed and board we saved on – that's more than £350 right there. She was worth a thousand and we got her for free. I wondered, *Is it an omen?*

When you buy a horse, especially a thoroughbred, you get a load of paperwork including what's called a 'stud book' saying who she is, where she's been and what medication she's had. It's her medical card, birth certificate and passport rolled into one. For bureaucratic reasons all horses are given the same birthday of 1 January in the year they were born. I don't know why. Someone must have thought it was a good idea once. The upshot is, it doesn't matter if they arrive at Christmas or on Valentine's Day, on paper they're all New Year babies. By that logic, Rewbell was born 1 January 1986 from a sire (father) called Andy Rew and a dam (mother) called Miss Bell. You can see the owners were imaginative with her name.

I poured over every detail in the paperwork. Seeing everything in black and white made it that much more real. After dinner I packed the lot up and set off for work at the club. I got lucky because who should be there already but Howard Davies. I walked right up to him, dumped all the literature on the bar and said, 'Right, I've bought the mare, I've done everything I said I would do. Now: yes or no, are you coming on board or not?'

He looked like I was asking for his kidney. Face contorted in anguish, hands wringing, head shaking, rocking back and forth on his stool – I thought he might be having a seizure. In truth, he did have a problem with his heart because it was slugging it out with his head. Half of him desperately wanted to get involved, half of him was too scared of being burned again financially. The torment the poor man was going through and I wasn't helping. I kept pushing and pushing.

'Look,' he said eventually, 'I don't know. I will have to ask my wife.'

Yes, I thought. *I've got him.*

From that moment I knew it was just a matter of time before Howard said yes officially. I felt if I worked on him properly he'd crumble sooner rather than later. I rang him every day after that, saying, 'Have you asked her? Have you asked your Angela?'

'No, no, I'm still thinking about it.'

That was a lie for a start. I knew full well he'd made up his mind already. He wanted nothing more than to get involved. He was just too scared of telling his missus.

Howard's passion for the horses was one of the reasons I was pulling up trees to get him on my team. That original conversation I'd earwigged on had been so enlightening. The man loved a bet, that was his entry point into the sport, but he also loved the animals themselves. You could hear it in his voice. He knew all about their ways and their needs. When he got involved with his original syndicate that was a dream come true. He loved his horse and was heartbroken when it got injured, bringing the venture to a close. Obviously he dreamed his horse would be a winner, but overwhelmingly he just loved being around it, being an insider in the sport.

'Howard,' I said, 'I can offer you all of that. You'll be an insider, you'll be as hands-on as you want to be – and I promise you, you'll be a winner as well.'

I had no reason to doubt myself, did I? I won everything I tried to win with the birds and the dogs. That was despite a lack of experience and not ever being, or wanting to be, part of the old boys' network. I felt I saw what was needed and I worked out, on my own, how to get it. It's like building with Lego. My grandson used to want this and that and I'd think, *Okay, how do I begin? What pieces do I need?* Life's quite simple if you let it be.

Every time Howard dared come into the club I cornered him. If a day or two went by without me bumping into him I'd ring him at home. The longer he procrastinated the more time I had to work out the details.

'Look,' I said one day, 'with twenty or thirty people we can do it for £10 a week. If you get people paying from the foal being born, he's not doing much for the first year, so there's not much in outgoings there. He'll get some training a bit later but he can't run till he's three so we'll mainly be putting money in the bank for a while.'

'What if we run out?' he asked. 'I'm not subsidizing another horse.'

'If we run out of investment we withdraw him and bring him home until we've brought a few more people in. No one's losing anything.'

I've never sold anything as hard in my life. My grand scheme, if you can call it that, was to breed a thoroughbred. That's as far as I thought. I could never afford to do it on my own. I'm mad, not stupid. The only way it could work was with Howard sorting out a syndicate. As the only person I'd ever met who'd done that, he was essential to my plan. He was my key Lego block. But if it didn't work out that wasn't the end of the world. I'd still get my foal and I would look after it myself. Brian would be over the moon. We just wouldn't go racing, that's all.

I don't know if Howard ever did mention it to his wife – he says he did but I have my doubts. Anyway, I got home one day, ready to hassle him again, and the answerphone was flashing 'one new message'. It was from him. He'd beaten me to it.

'Don't bother calling me tonight, Janet. I give up. I'm in.'

Obviously I had to call him after that, didn't I?

'First things first,' Howard said, 'we need to gauge interest. Let's start local. We'll put up a notice in the club – if that's all right with you, Mrs Manager – and see if anybody's up for it. Let's look at what we get and we'll take it from there.'

So that's what we did.

We wrote on the notice that there'd be a meeting upstairs in the club on a certain date. We tried to make it as appealing as possible but at the end of the day we'd be asking strangers to give money to a project run by amateurs in a demanding closed shop of a sport populated by millionaires and kings. With very good reason, I worried that no one would turn up.

'Their loss,' Brian said. 'But you know what people are like. You only need one person to set the ball rolling.'

In the end we got five. We had Gerwyn Evans – a fella who drank in the club. There was Kevin French, Alan Baldwin, Carl Lewis and Howard himself. With Brian and me that wasn't a terrible start.

Howard did most of the talking, obviously. He started by explaining how our syndicate would differ from the regular set-up. For a start, the big organizations usually buy in the finished article – some horse that a trainer recommends with a bright future. And not just one. They get in dozens because they have so many members. Each punter pays a one-off fee of £100 or £250, whatever, and at the end of the season not only do they get a slice of the winnings but they also get a share of the sell-on fee that each of those horses earns. The following season they buy new horses and do it all over again. Members can go the whole year not knowing, meeting or caring about the individual horses. They are just numbers on a spreadsheet. It's all about the cash.

'That's the normal way,' Howard said. 'But that's not what we're proposing.'

Our approach was cradle to the grave. 'It is my dream,' I said, 'my ambition, to breed a thoroughbred horse, one capable of winning races. For that I need your help. I can't afford to do it alone. So what I propose is: I will supply the mare and the stud and I will breed the foal and I will let you, the syndicate, have it for what it costs me to breed. Basically the stud fee. After that, you will pay a weekly sum for its upkeep and care. You will all own the horse. You will all be able to call it your own. You can visit it, decide every aspect of its life or just sit back and wait for the winnings. This can be whatever you want it to be.'

'That sounds very fair,' they all said. 'Is there a catch?'

'There's no catch,' I said, 'but when the horse finishes

racing, when you don't need it any more, it comes back to me. I want its last home to be here among friends.'

'What about a sell-on?' That was one of the more astute questions.

'If it's a colt the horse will be gelded,' I said. 'He'll have no value after he hangs up his hooves. If it's a mare then possibly there's value if she breeds. All I care about is giving it a good home.'

We were a small group but everyone was in agreement. I was doing the lion's share of the work, I was the one breeding the horse and I was the one most concerned about its welfare. I was the engine, if you like. No one would put more care into his or her retirement so they said yes. 'The horse is yours at the end. That seems reasonable.'

I wish I'd got that in writing. The truth is, I was so excited to see the syndicate beginning to take shape I wasn't thinking of things like small print.

Speaking of details, Howard then explained how our syndicate would work. They'd need to contribute a certain amount every week to pay for the horse's care and then at the end of its racing career any and all winnings would be divided equally among the investors. It all sounded very straightforward. All decisions on the horse's future would be taken by the group, decided on a show of hands. It wasn't my toy or Howard's toy. Our syndicate would be a proper, genuine community project. No bosses, no underlings. All votes would be equal.

For that reason I decided not to become a member. I thought with me breeding the horse and selling it to the syndicate the relationship could get a bit messy. I thought Brian should join on behalf of the family, pay his subscription and give our say and I'd remain in the background.

What a mistake that was as well. I just didn't know it yet.

The truth is, if I could change one decision I've made in my life it would be that one. But at the time it made sense and, by the end of the meeting, we all felt positive. Nothing could happen till our numbers had swollen considerably though. The feeling was that a decent amount of people probably couldn't be persuaded to part with their pound notes until there was an actual horse that they could see with their own eyes. In other words, they were all waiting for me.

September came and with it one of the happiest days of my life. Brian and I drove out with an empty horse box and returned with a full one. No more waiting, no more delays, no more excuses. Rewbell was finally ours.

As valuable as she was to my plans she didn't get any special treatment. We did with her what we'd done with all Brian's horses. We took her to the allotment.

There aren't many positives to come out of the mines closing down but that patch of land a mile from our house is categorically one of them. Years ago it would have been part of one of the largest slag heaps in the country. When the Britannia Colliery closed down, the tip stopped being used, nature found a way through as she always does, and grass eventually sprouted. Fast forward and it's on top of that very sludge hill that we have a patch of land 50ft x 100ft, just like the one my father shared with his brother. The difference is, unlike his allotment and all the others around us that are filled with neat rows of beans and potatoes and carrots, Brian and I don't use our space to grow vegetables. There's no point. They'd get eaten by what we *do* grow: horses.

At least that was the plan.

I was so pleased to finally get Rewbell under our stable roof. Brian asked me if I wanted to ride her but I couldn't. I had big dreams for her but none of them included me having a gallop.

'This girl's got enough to do without lugging me around.'

Obviously the plan was to get Rewbell impregnated but I didn't want to rush anything. It didn't seem right. She'd only just finished suckling her last foal. Brian advised, 'Give her at least six months, maybe even a year, to get settled in, get her used to us. It'll pay off in the long run.'

I bowed to his superior knowledge on the subject but I had another reason for agreeing. Despite all the detailed Dos and Don'ts in the documents I'd received with her purchase I had to admit to myself, *I have absolutely no idea how to go about getting her foaled.*

'Phone Ron,' Brian said. 'He'll hold your hand.'

When we were without a horse, Brian used to go up to Shirley Williams' farm in Markham and ride one of hers. She bred Welsh cobs, all sorts, and won prizes with many of them. What she didn't know about horses hardly anyone did. The exception was a fella called Ron. He used to be one of the busiest vets around. I say 'used to' because he was already retired when we met him. But he still kept his hand in the business, often for no money. 'Giving something back to the community,' he used to say. He'd have surgeries up at Shirley's farm every so often and anyone with an animal problem could fetch the creature up there and he'd have a look. He never charged for his time, only for any medication he might have to dispense. That's where Brian had met him years before, while riding Shirley's horses.

So I rang Ron and he talked me through the logistics. First of all, he said, I needed to find a stallion. Then Rewbell would have to be tested for all sorts of diseases, especially of the venereal kind. Ron offered to do that – take swabs, run the blood work, all of it. Without these tests no stud farm would accept a mare. 'You'll be signing so much paperwork it's not worth taking a risk,' he said.

Then came the tricky bit. 'You have to bring her into season.'

Like I said, all horses are given the same birthday of

1 January regardless of when they're born in a year. For racing purposes, he said you want to have a foal as early in the calendar year as possible. That way he's stronger than all the others his age. You can't race a horse in the UK over hurdles before three years old and most people try to get going as close to that day as possible. If you've got a colt or filly that's closer to two than three in calendar terms you're going to struggle against those with an extra eleven months under their belts. That's the theory anyway.

You'd think these things would all be left up to Mother Nature but no. It wasn't just access to the stallions that owners had control over. You could also help the mare come into season. Left to her own devices that would normally naturally occur in spring. The warmer weather, the longer days, they all contribute to the mare's body deciding it's the time to start a family. But, if you get her covered – that is, impregnated – in April or May or June you won't be looking at getting a foal until eleven months after, so you'll be losing that edge over the competition.

'It's up to you,' Ron said, 'but you can make the mare come into season early by tricking her into thinking it's spring.'

'How on earth do you do that without taking her to Spain? Have you noticed the weather we have over here?'

'It's a bit time-consuming but it works.'

So how do you trick a mare into thinking it's spring, not winter? You have to get a load of lights around the stable for a start. As soon as the nights start drawing in towards the end of the year you put your lamps on till about 10.30 at night. Then first thing the following morning, 5.30 or 6, you go up and switch them on again. You also cut the mare's food down from September to December. Not to starve them by any means, but reduce it. Then from 1 December you up their measures again and with the added lights they think it is spring.

As Ron was telling me all this I was thinking, *Blimey, it's not that complicated getting a dog pregnant.*

As we'd discussed, we wanted to give Rewbell a bit of a rest before we got her working again. I figured if she wasn't comfortable in her new surroundings then it wasn't going to help our chances of getting a foal out of her. Better to work with her than against her. Like most women I suppose.

There was no rush then in finding a stud. That didn't mean I wasn't looking as soon as I was pointed in the right direction. On Howard's advice I got hold of the *Directory of the Turf* – the thoroughbred industry's bible – and whiled away whole days comparing this horse to that. It's a weird thing to be doing. It's a bit like ordering a takeaway, although a darned sight more expensive. You see a picture, you see the ingredients and you have to decide if you fancy it or not. But, as I always say, you can't beat actually visiting the restaurant.

My favourite potential suitor was at Kirtlington Stud,

over Oxford way. According to their website they were the first stud farm in England to foal, raise and consign a world champion. So that sounded like a place we needed to go, didn't it? The stallion that caught my eye was called Blushing Flame. I liked him a lot in the book; he was even better in the flesh. He ticked all our boxes, especially for pedigree. Rewbell was thirteen at the time and her racing history was the sort you'd cover your eyes to read through the cracks in your fingers. I'm not saying she didn't have potential, she just didn't like racing. She certainly didn't like anyone on her back; the boy we bought her from made that clear enough and her record backed it up. As far as I can work out, she saw her mission in life was to unseat any jockey who dared line her up. She was spirited, let's say that.

Just as important, Blushing Flame also fell within my budget. He was going to cost £1,500 + VAT for his services. On top of that you had to be prepared to pay for however many nights the mare stayed until the dirty deed was done. If the stallion doesn't like the look of her or he's not in the mood it could take a while.

You have to get everything signed in triplicate before they let you anywhere near one of their stallions, and that's before you get the medical examinations done. It took me ages to wade through every detail but finally I got it sent off. I was expecting copies back in the post any day. Instead I got a phone call.

'We've got some bad news, Mrs Vokes,' they said.

'It's not Blushing Flame, is it? He's not ill, is he?'

'No, he's healthy enough. It's just he has had enough bookings so he's moving to stud in France. Do you want us to make arrangements to send Rewbell over there?'

A romantic weekend in France might be the height of human fantasy but what we were negotiating was a bit less lovey-dovey.

'I'll be honest,' I said, 'I like the horse but it's not make or break for me. Our mare isn't worth a lot of money and it's all a bit of a gamble whether we're doing the right thing full stop.'

'In that case,' they said, 'we've got a new stallion coming in fresh from America. He retails at £3,000 but we'll let you have him for £2,000 if you want.'

It was a fair price but more than we'd budgeted.

'I'll have to take a look, won't I?'

I'm so glad I did. The horse was called Bien Bien and he was and still is the ten furlong record holder at California's Hollywood Park, so on paper he was spot on. In the flesh he was even more perfect if that's possible. I thought Blushing Flame was handsome but if you had them side by side in a stable you'd only pick Bien Bien. He was chestnut, like Rewbell, and he was proud. I could see them making a beautiful couple for a few minutes – and an even more beautiful foal.

Like so many other things in my life, Blushing Flame dropping out was another episode which sounded like bad news at the time but actually shaped my future in a very, very positive way. Things happen for a reason, don't they? Even if you do get your first choice horse, the variables in breeding are monstrous. When we were breeding the whippets there was always one standout pup in the litter that came out exactly as you hoped for from the genes of the parents we put together. The rest, in varying degrees, were less successful if you like. And, don't forget, with dogs we were mainly going on looks, not abilities. Apart from the process being cheaper and easier, bitches have an extra advantage of having half a dozen or more babies. A mare, generally, only has one at a time so the pressure on the mix and matching was greater. But I'd done what I could. I felt Bien Bien's pedigree and abilities complemented Rewbell's as well as anybody's could. I thought she would give the guts and staying power and perhaps the personality and he would supply the speed and strength. You'd have to be very lucky to get a horse fast enough for flat course racing, but if everything went to plan I'd have something capable of holding its own over jumps. That was best-case scenario.

We bought Rewbell in 1998 and by 2000 I felt she was ready to meet her man. We got Ron doing all the blood work and getting her certified medically and when we estimated she was naturally in season we made the booking. Finally, in March we headed down the M40 to Kirtlington for our girl's date with her toy boy.

'They'd better have some iron in his diet,' Brian said.

It's always a slow journey with the horse box so you have extra time to think and worry. By this stage our little syndicate-in-the-making had about seven committed members. Including Howard, only three of them were at the original meeting, so two had dropped out. We wouldn't officially be up and running until the foal was born or we reached twenty-five members. Any less than that and Howard reckoned we wouldn't contribute enough money between us to pay for training and everything that competing in races demands. If that was the case Brian and I had already talked about just keeping the foal as our pet. Part of me was okay with that. The other part was itching to prove myself on the equine circuit. I was desperate for Howard to get some more members. I really wanted to make it work.

We arrived at the yard just outside Oxford, got the horse settled into her stable then went to the office with all the paperwork. It should all have been a formality but the fella in charge looked at the horse and at the blood tests and said because Rewbell presented with some discharge we'd need to wait another cycle.

That wasn't a great start. Bearing in mind on top of the stud fee we had to pay £13 + VAT bed and board every day Rewbell was there, I began to worry about funds.

I had to pay for everything somehow even though there was no money coming in, so I'd raided mine and Brian's joint savings account – and never told him. Every bill that came in was settled out of there. It was another reason why I was so anxious for Howard to get the syndicate off the ground.

The regimen we had administered to bring Rewbell into season was another cost to bear. With the second load of bloodwork it was all adding up. It would have been tolerable if our girl had been covered in the first week. But after seven days nothing had happened. Same story the following week. A fortnight later I'd had enough. We'd been to visit and in my opinion Rewbell wasn't looking her best so I couldn't see her breeding any time soon. On 5 April I rang the stud and said, 'Knock it on the head. I'm coming to collect her.'

It wasn't a case of 'can we afford it?', it was more 'is it worth it?'. The mare was of no consequence in the grand scheme of things, she had no racing pedigree as such behind her. We were haemorrhaging money, and for what? A silly woman's vanity project. That's what it felt like at that moment.

'Don't be so hasty,' they said. 'Give us a couple more days.'

'I don't know.'

'What have you got to lose?'

'A load more bloody money for a start.'

'Two days,' they said.

'Okay.'

Forty-eight hours later, on 7 April as promised, they rang back.

'Congratulations, Mrs Vokes. Your mare was covered

successfully this morning. She's been stitched and everything looks fine. You can collect her tomorrow.'

Such a relief. To have my Rewbell coming home was great but her in foal as well was the icing on the cake.

I also swore to myself that if I ever did this again I'd do it differently. I'd take Ron's advice and only send the mare to be covered when we were sure she was in season. *Still*, I thought, *life's a learning curve. You're allowed to make mistakes. How else are you going to improve?*

That's what I told myself, anyway. My bank manager might have been less understanding . . .

Kirtlington played fair with the stud fee. The rule was, you don't pay a penny until October. By then you'd know if the cover had been successful. No foal, no fee.

It also allowed time for unfortunate accidents to be spotted. It was clear to Ron that Rewbell had taken, but to be on the safe side, and before we parted with any (more) money, he said, 'We'll do a scan in September. Put your minds at rest before you have to pay.'

Like I say, apart from his community work Ron was pretty much retired. Once he'd had a full surgical operating theatre at his home but he'd long since got rid of that when we arrived. He still had the equipment for scanning though. There was a stable with two metal bars set into the concrete. You had to lead your horse between them so it couldn't kick out while it was being examined.

Brian took the lead rope and led Rewbell in. Ron took up the rear, literally it turned out. While I stood in the middle in front of a computer screen he'd set up, Ron was snapping on a long, long glove and arming himself with what looked like a pen on a wire.

'Are you ready?' he asked.

'Definitely,' I said.

'Okay, Brian, hold her steady now. I'm going in.'

And with that his arm and the pen began to disappear inside the mare's rectum. The pen Ron was holding was an ultrasound. A similar process is used on human females to get an image of the foetus, but with one exception – the exploratory process is conducted outside the body. It was proper James Herriot stuff. I had to look away. Lucky I did because suddenly the computer screen fuzzed into life.

I was getting anxious and excited at the same time. There was something on the screen but it was too blurry to make out. As Ron moved his sonar pen up and down the image changed and changed until suddenly I said, 'Ron, go back! Go back to where you were.'

'Here?' he asked.

'Bit further.'

'Here?'

'Yes! Yes! I can see it. I can see the foal.'

And I could. Oh my God. I hadn't been that happy since the scans for my own children.

'Are you crying?' Brian called out.

'What if I am? It's beautiful.'

You know when you well up when you see a baby? It

was exactly the same looking at this foal. It was so tiny, more like a sea horse than a real horse, but it brought tears to my eyes. *That's it*, I thought, *I'm in love. You're mine. You're coming home with me.*

I was mesmerized by the image on the screen. I couldn't take my eyes off it. Not that I was any use.

'Janet,' Ron called out, 'can you tell the sex?'

'No, I don't think so. What am I looking for?'

As soon as the words came out of my mouth I regretted it.

Brian leapt on my gaffe, of course he did. 'You know, love, horses have this reputation . . .'

Unfortunately, Ron didn't have any paper in his printer so we couldn't get a copy of the scan. Unless I wanted to swap places with him, he couldn't see the onscreen image either. But we could hear the heartbeat and that sounded strong as you like. There was a poetry to the rhythmic pulsing that made me weak at the knees.

I was a nervous wreck by the time we left. And not just because I'd seen my precious baby. With everything looking wonderfully normal I'd have to pay £2,000 in a week's time.

Where am I going to get that kind of money? Sorry, Brian . . .

Not knowing the gender didn't bother me unduly. Each sex has its pros and cons. If you have a good winning filly, a fantastic one, they are worth more money than a colt because they can be sold as brood mares. The boys, on the other hand, are gelded nine times out of ten so there's no follow-on value there. At the end of their race career they are just riding horses. But in the short term, boys are more powerful so they do tend to win races. It's very rare a filly will beat a colt.

The gestation period for a horse is eleven to twelve months, so by our maths Rewbell was due to give birth the third week of March 2001. With any pregnancy in any species there is a bit of leeway one way or the other. To be on the safe side we shipped her over to the stable at Ron's in good time. After that it was just waiting for his call. Every morning I got up and looked at the phone. If it was flashing I had missed a call. Every time I left the house, the first thing I did when I came back was stare at that handset. Nothing flashing, no news. Same old story every day. I was doing it out of habit in the end. Then on 24 March, I was out shopping, buying the same old rubbish, nothing out of the ordinary. I came home and dumped my bags down in the hallway. Something was on my mind, I can't remember what, but I do remember I didn't look immediately at the phone. When I did it was by accident. Something had caught my attention out of the corner of my eye.

It was the phone. It was flashing.

It's funny, you spend so many days expecting something and when it comes you just imagine all the other things it could be. Was it Dennis phoning me? Or my grandson? Maybe it was Sasha telling me she would be home late. When I pressed play I had no expectations.

'Hello Jan.' It was Ron's voice, unmistakable. I held my breath. What was he going to say? 'Just ringing to tell you, your mare has foaled.'

Oh my God.

'It is a colt, it's perfect, but the most important thing is your vet needs sleep! On no account visit for at least another four hours. Or else!'

I played that tape over and over and when Brian came in I played it twice more again. 'I've got to get round there,' I said.

'You heard the man, you can't. He's been up all night.'

'But we've got a baby. I've got to see him.'

I tell you, those four hours were up by barely a second and we swung into Ron's driveway. Howard and Kevin French from the syndicate weren't far behind. We hovered outside for ages not knowing what to do with ourselves, then a very bleary-eyed vet led us to the stables.

'You've got a special one there, I can tell,' he said. 'Trust me, I've seen a lot of foals in here and right from the go, he's got something about him.'

I wasn't really in any frame of mind to listen at the time. I was so anxious to see the new addition to my family. But I played his words back repeatedly later. I'd looked for an omen earlier; was this the one I craved?

We got inside and I thought I was going to die with

happiness. There he was, this spindly, gorgeous creature, lying on the floor so peaceful next to his mum. As soon as he saw us he staggered to his feet, alert and wary. Brian went straight over to have a pet and he kicked out. Me, Howard and Kevin would have run for the hills. Brian stood his ground and grinned.

'Oh, he's got some spirit this one. What do you think?'

I'll tell you what I thought: he was perfect. He was chestnut, of course, like both his parents. On his legs he had four white socks so identical you'd think they were painted on. (His dad, Bien Bien, only had them on two.) Horses' legs don't develop below the knee – what they're born with is what they keep – so that amazing feature would never change. On top of that there was a blaze of white on his forehead. No doubt about it, I was in love. And I was ready to do anything.

'He's perfect, Brian,' I said.

'You're not wrong.'

He was as smitten as I was. While Howard and Kevin were over with Ron, I said, 'I don't think I can do it.'

'Do what?'

'Give him away.'

'What are you talking about,' he said. 'You've made an agreement. You've got a syndicate waiting for you.'

'I don't care.' It was a struggle to keep my voice down. 'It doesn't matter what I've said. Nothing is signed, no one has paid nothing. This foal is mine. He's coming home with me.'

7

Lost Youth

We'd been there half an hour and nothing had changed. Howard and Kevin were still bending Ron's ear and I was doing the same to my husband. 'Brian,' I said, 'I don't know about this. I'm not sure I can give him up.'

'Come on,' he said, 'he's a beauty for sure, but us two can't afford to get him racing on our own.'

He had a quandary then for sure. This man had loved horses for longer than I'd been alive. But he also loved me.

'What about your dream of breeding a thoroughbred winner?'

'Come on, lots of people say things they don't really believe.'

'But you know I believe in you, right? If you say you can do it, I think you can.'

'Do you really?'

'Yes, I do. But you have to give up Ianto.'

'Oh, Ianto now, is it?'

Whatever horse was in our stables we used to call either Ianto or Dai Bando – characters from the film *How Green Was My Valley*. Ianto was played by John Loder and Dai Bando by Rhys Williams.

'Don't you think he looks like a Ianto?' Brian said.

'I suppose he does.'

'Anyway, whatever his name is you have to honour your commitment.'

Of course he was right. He usually is. That didn't stop me hurting, even as I walked back over to Howard.

'You've seen the foal,' I said. 'He's a beauty and a champion, I can tell. Now it's your turn. You need to get this syndicate off the ground or I'm taking my ball home with me.'

It's true I owed it to everyone to honour my commitment. But I wasn't going to let that ride without making another promise. Not to Howard, not to Brian or even myself. It was to Ianto, my new baby.

Rewbell was exhausted but lovely and she let me walk up to her son and even touch him.

'Listen, young man,' I said, 'I want to make you a deal. You've already given me so much pleasure just standing there. But I'm going to train you, lad, I'm going to give you everything I can to make you a champion. So here's the thing: if you give me everything, if you try your hardest and live up to the potential I believe you have, if you help me achieve my dream, then when you're done I promise I will bring you home. You'll come back to me, you'll come back to your mother, and we'll spoil you rotten. Is that a deal?'

I'm not saying he nodded, I'm not even saying he heard. But that was the pledge I made to him. Those were the words that I swore to live by.

I'd done everything I could. Now it was Howard's turn.

Although only three of the original five who'd expressed interest in the syndicate had stayed the course, Howard had got others: Derek and Christine Brunnock, Mike Davey and Gordon Hogg. They all came aboard. As soon as Ianto was born Howard really pulled his finger out and went canvassing around the local tax office the next day at work. When that well ran dry he turned to his own family. Within a couple of weeks we had nearly twenty names. It was time to call a meeting.

We got everyone together and Howard as syndicate leader went through the whys and wherefores of the agreement. Minutes were taken, it was as official as we could manage, and financial commitments were made. Everyone agreed to pay £10 a week, roughly £40 a month. If you missed three months you were out. That was the understanding. Holidays or a rough few weeks shouldn't be enough to ruin your investment and after three months we figured you should have yourself sorted. Anyone who hadn't paid during that time was taking the mickey.

Howard obviously ran the show and Kevin French, who had come to visit Ianto after he was born, was nominated as syndicate secretary. He used to run the business centre in the town and also freelanced as the finance secretary of the working men's club so I knew him and his abilities. I'm not convinced he thanked us for the extra responsibility but as the only accountant on the team he was the obvious choice. He did the accounts for us for free every year. He printed everything out, gave everybody a copy, and he accounted for every penny – not easy when there was so much cash involved.

I was the person paying most of the bills for Ianto's upkeep so keeping track of things was harder for me. Usually I'd have paid cash if I had it without thinking, but Kevin explained how even if I wanted to buy a five pound bale of hay I had to raise an invoice with him and he'd draft a cheque from the syndicate account. Whatever we did, there needed to be an inscrutable paper trail.

'It seems like a lot of hassle, for you more than anyone. Can't you just take my word?'

'I can,' he said, 'but you've got nineteen other people who might question where the pennies go.'

'They'll be fine,' I said, 'they're either friends of mine or friends of Howard's. They know how it is. They know I wouldn't cheat them.'

'Let me give you a bit of free advice, Janet, if I may. I've worked in finance all my life and one thing I've learned is that where money is concerned friendship doesn't come into it. Neither does family either, some-times, more's the pity. You owe it to yourself more than anyone to be visibly doing the right thing or someone will kick up. They always do.'

I called him an old doom-monger of course but I heeded the words. There's no point employing experts and ignoring their advice. While the more businesslike members of the syndicate set up direct debits into Ianto's account, others preferred to hand me their forty quid every month when they bumped into me in the club. I had to then bank this cash and get a receipt. It didn't matter if I had some feed to buy for exactly that amount, I had to first pay in their contributions then get the cash separately from Kevin before I could spend a penny. Unless it showed on the bank statement it didn't happen.

'Trust me,' Kevin said, 'some people will already be begrudging you getting their money . . .' My personal deal with the syndicate was straightforward enough. I was the breeder and I'd pledged to let them have the foal as long as I wasn't out of pocket. I didn't charge a fee for the horse, I didn't sell him to them as such, I just asked that my costs of insemination, stabling, vet bills and the like were recompensed. So that, it was agreed, was where the lion's share of the first year's subs would go. I made out that I wasn't fussed how long it took but, honestly, every day I was owed was another day that Brian might notice his account was down. I have to say, it was all paid back when Kevin said it would be and Brian was none the wiser. Until he reads this!

And, despite Kevin's foreboding, I never heard a

member of the syndicate complain. But then, I wasn't a member, was I?

Finances, debts and procedures don't really float my boat. All I really cared about that March was getting my Ianto and Rewbell home. As soon as Ron the vet gave the all-clear, we went down with our old horse box and popped them aboard. The next bit of land Ianto saw would become the stuff of legend. Not that we had even an inkling at the time.

Watching Brian lead them onto the allotment gave me such a sense of pride. Rewbell was such a good mother. As sore as she must still have been, if she'd thought Brian was doing anything wrong she'd have intervened, no question. As it was, she could sense he was trying to help her boy so she let it happen, although staying never more than a yard away.

I got the stables looking as nice as I could. It wasn't the most deluxe of accommodations – Brian had fixed most of it at one time or another – but it was roomy, water-proof and kept the wind out. They had fresh hay, fresh water, they were brushed daily and mucked out morning and night. Apart from a morning paper I couldn't think what else we could offer.

For the first few days Ianto never left his mum's side. When she ventured outdoors he followed, nuzzling her all the time. After a week or so he got a bit spritelier and started trotting off as best he could, but always popping back for his milk. About two weeks in he started nibbling at some hay and I knew he was on his way. Much of this Brian reported back to me but a lot of it I saw with my own eyes. I swear I had the imprint of the gate to our allotment moulded into me I was hanging off it that much. It honestly felt like when I'd had my Dennis and Sacha. I just couldn't bear to be away. I wanted to catch every development.

By a month old he was taking on as much grass as he was milk. And to think where that grass was coming from. I remember standing with Brian, saying, 'Can you believe, fifty years ago this was a slag heap. You'd be lucky to get rats up here, let alone a horse.'

'I miss those days,' he said. 'I always thought the pits were so beautiful.'

'So did I. But you know, for all the fun we had playing on them that lad is getting a lot more out of it.'

We weren't the only ones hanging off the gate. I have to say, virtually every member of the syndicate came down to check on their investment. Some of them had never seen a horse outside of a bookies' television screen. Even fewer had touched one. I must admit to mixed feelings at first. A fella I knew and liked strolled over next to me and said, matter of fact, 'So that's my horse, is it?'

I wanted to grab him by the neck: 'No, he's not *your* horse. He's *mine*.'

I never expected it to be so hard to take. But I'd done

the deal, I was taking the money, they were paying me back. We were all in it together.

As long as people were gentle, Brian would lead Ianto over to have a pat and a stroke. As he got older, Brian would take him over the road to the field he'd rented for his horses as long as I'd known him. Watching Ianto bomb around like a headless chicken didn't particularly fill anyone with confidence that he'd do anything special. But then, apparently not everyone expected him to.

We were standing there one day and I overheard a couple of lads, good men, loyal syndicate members, and they were saying, 'As long as we get at least one free day at the races I'll be happy.'

'I'm just glad to have something to do,' the other one said. 'And what else would bring all these people together?'

I hadn't looked at it like that before. I was so wrapped up in Ianto himself and, before that, my crazy plot to mount an assault on the sport of kings, I hadn't noticed how the syndicate was actually bringing people together. And not just members either. Ianto was barely two months old and I couldn't go into a shop without a member of staff or a customer asking me, 'How's your champion coming along, Janet?'

People were just interested. I don't know why. No one cared about the pigeons or the dogs. All I know is, the horse got everyone's attention and it hadn't even done anything yet. Not only that, it didn't even have a name.

'Ianto' was all well and good but, to be honest, the amount of Iantos I've seen over the years would fill a phonebook.

For racing purposes he needed something more, something official. With the whippets we went a bit crazy with Romantic Notions, but King Of The Road, Rags To Riches and Pinball Wizard had sounded more horsey. I thought, *If I put my mind to it I can come up with a belter.*

Then I had a word with myself. I had to, didn't I?

It's not your decision, Janet Vokes. You have to let the syndicate decide.

This arrangement was going to take some getting used to.

There was such a buzz about the project that those early meetings were more often than not conducted in a pub or restaurant. Yes, the meeting was all official and minuted and everyone voted when necessary, but we didn't want to forget to have some fun along the way.

On the agenda this particular day were two important topics: the first was lunch, the second was the horse's name. The plan was pretty simple. Everyone had to write a name on a piece of paper, we'd put them in a hat, then as they were read out anonymously we'd have a show of hands on each one. As I wasn't an official member of the syndicate I wasn't sure if they'd let me contribute a choice but Howard insisted I did and if anyone had a problem with it they didn't voice it. It was very kind of him. The only problem was, I didn't have a clue what to write down. Thinking I wouldn't have a vote, I hadn't put much thought into it beforehand.

While he was at the bar I said to Howard, 'I've got nothing. What are you going for?'

He said, 'I really like Dream Alliance. It sort of sums up everything we're trying to do here. This alliance of strangers is helping us achieve our dream.'

'That's a lovely name, that is.'

'Or,' he continued, 'I was also thinking about Lost Youth. We're none of us getting any younger, are we, but I think this horse will give us all an injection of what we've left behind.'

Two amazing names. Great stories as well. I loved them both.

'Which do you prefer?' I said.

'At a push I'd go for Dream Alliance.'

'Okay then, I'll write down Lost Youth.'

'Actually,' he said, 'maybe you could write down Dream Alliance instead. There's one or two who think I'm a bit power mad so they won't vote for anything I suggest just to be cantankerous.'

Half an hour later I was disappointed to see he was right. Early suggestions like 'Power Gem' and 'Red Robin' roused a couple of people each and a few outright stupid ones were thrown away, but when 'Lost Youth' came out the hat there were more than a handful of positive noises. Then Howard let slip it was his idea, which was either a naive or very clever thing to do because by the time the show of hands happened, those positive noises didn't translate into as many votes as I initially expected. I looked round the room at the people I assumed were all in it together and thought, *Maybe Howard has a point about people out to get him.*

'Lost Youth' being shot down meant that when 'Dream Alliance' was read out, no one who had an axe to grind with Howard played silly beggars. It was such a popular choice we didn't bother looking at the others.

'That's us,' someone said, 'we're the Dream Alliance.'

'I'll drink to that,' Brian said. 'To us, the Dream Alliance.'

8

I'm Here About the Jockey's Job

Some of my shifts at the working men's club involved pretty unsociable hours. On the plus side, it did give me quite a lot of daylight hours to myself. So where did I spend them?

I don't think there was a colt in the world who had a coat brushed as often as 'Dream', as he was now called. Once I'd helped Brian clean out the stable and sort the feed, I'd just stand there with my brush and the colt would let me groom him. By six months he was beginning to get some independence from his mother and she was happy to let him. Some mares don't like you touching their babies but Rewbell was never like that. As long as we treated him right, I suppose, it was all right by her. And I promise, no horse could have been loved more.

As Dream got stronger Brian let him have longer running in the field opposite the allotment. I went down one day and stood by the gate as usual, just happy watching.

He was a typical boy. Happy eating one minute then bolting off for no reason the next.

Spirited, I thought, *like his mother.*

Standing still he was gorgeous, running around he was a vision. His tail and his head were high and proud. As mad as he looked darting and twirling and sprinting and stopping suddenly, I could feel him pushing himself, exploring what he was capable of.

After a while he stopped gadding around and began trotting over in my direction. I thought he might want to go back in the stable. That would be a first, so then I began to worry he might be feeling unwell. I watched as he came closer and closer to the gate. He stopped in front of me and stretched out his neck and pushed his beautiful big head into my shoulder.

Oh, you just want a stroke!

I welled up, of course I did. I started pouring my heart out to him. All my worries, all my troubles, and I swear his ears pricked up right from the start.

'You're listening, aren't you?' I said.

I'd always believed he was special and there was the proof. When I finished going on and on, he gave a little harrumph, stamped his white feet then skedaddled back into the field.

That's what life's about, isn't it? Magical moments.

Another regular visitor to the allotment of course was Howard. Like me, he was thrilled enough just to stand there. He'd be there sometimes when I'd arrive, lost in his own world.

'Penny for your thoughts, Howard?'

'Oh, hello Janet. Just dreaming of what might be, you know.'

'It won't be a dream for long,' I said.

He laughed. 'You really believe that, don't you?'

'I wouldn't have started all this if I didn't. The plan was to breed a racehorse. You're looking at the horse part. All that's missing now is a race.'

'You make it sound so simple.'

'No I don't,' I said. 'Everyone else just makes things sound too difficult. Look: we've got a goal, we've got as much right as anyone to succeed. Just because that boy is running around an old slag heap doesn't mean he's not capable of greatness. There's no rule that says racehorses have to be owned by sheikhs and millionaires. We're going to show them a thing or two, Howard Davies, I promise you that.'

I don't know if he shared my faith but he was content enough to enjoy the ride. He put so much effort into researching every stage of our plan, always one step ahead of everyone else. Whenever I needed to chat about what to do, first I'd go to Dream himself, then I'd go to Howard. We were a good team.

When Dream was born I signed up with the Thorough-bred Breeders Association. I had to get him his own stud book and registered. I had to fill in his sire and dam and what they'd achieved and everything. When it came to 'breeder' I wrote down the 'Rewbell Syndicate, care of Janet Vokes'. I could have just put my own name but I wanted to reflect I was part of a group whilst still being credited as breeder – which I was. As owner of the horse I wrote in the 'Alliance Syndicate' – the name we'd given ourselves. The two were similar but very crucially different.

All Ron's treatments also had to go in the book. I hoped we wouldn't be making another medical entry for a while but when Dream was about ten months the book came out again. The problem was, not all his visitors were as interested in his well-being as me, Howard and Brian. There was an empty field the other side of ours where the local lads used to play football. I used to see them even before Dream was born. The younger kids were all right. They'd be noisy enough, as kids are, but they minded their own business. It was the older boys who wanted everyone to know they were there. They'd bomb along the mud path to the allotments on their motorbikes, making all the noise in the world, and for a few minutes it was like a little army descending on you. Then they'd get to their field and you could forget about them until ninety minutes later when they did it all again going home.

One day, in February 2002, they didn't go straight home. I wasn't there. One of the gardeners in his patch saw it all. He said the lads went over to Dream's field and they were trying to get him to run. They'd be quiet for a period then make their motorcycles scream to try to get Dream to panic.

Which is exactly what he did. He ran off and one of them chased him along the perimeter of the fence. Before the gardener could get down there to put a stop to it, it was already too late. Dream had run straight into the barbed wire fence.

Our neighbour rang me immediately and told me to get over there. 'Hurry,' he said, 'his leg is in tatters.'

By the time I got there Ron was already on his way. I was relieved to see Dream standing. As I ran over to the horse I could see one of his pure white socks had turned red. I felt sick. He was obviously in distress but I didn't know whether it was from the pain or being tormented by those idiots. I calmed him down as best as I could and tried to have a look at the leg. There was so much blood. Him being too damaged to ever race never entered my head. I just wanted him to be all right.

When Ron arrived Dream was as cool as a cucumber and I was the one in turmoil. I held the horse while the vet did his work. I was no expert on horse treatment but everyone knows what happens if they lose the use of one of their legs.

Part of me didn't want to know but I had to ask, 'How bad is it, Ron?'

'You know what,' he said, 'I don't think it's as bad as

it looks. He's torn the skin, maybe a bit deeper, that's all. We'll get some cream and a bandage and he'll heal in no time.'

I could have kissed him. But first I had some young lads to throttle – and some big decisions to make.

I reported to Howard what had happened. 'I think it's time to think about moving him,' I said. 'I know we're going to have to pay for it but he needs to be somewhere a bit more protected.'

'Don't worry about the money. That's what the syndicate's for.'

I went back to my copy of the *Directory of the Turf* and started going through local places before spreading my search further afield. I'm not one of those people who pick the first thing they find. Just like when I was looking for stud dogs and stallions, I combed through each page forensically, weighing up the pros and cons of everyone. Eventually I found a place out in Hereford that looked like it would work.

Brian and I used to think nothing of driving to Manchester or London or Southampton for the dogs and birds so hopping over to Hereford was like a little reminder of those gallivanting days. If we were lucky, and our new hobby went the way of the others, it would be the first of many days out.

Christopher and Jackie Traitline ran a small stud farm over the border in Vowchurch and I was immediately impressed by their set-up. It was big enough to be professional and small enough for them to be able to keep on top of every single detail. They were a lovely couple and very upfront. They introduced us to Jane, who'd been working with the horses since she was a girl. She'd be the one taking care of Dream if he went there. I was very impressed with her. For £70 a week I thought Dream couldn't have gone into better hands.

The extra distance meant I couldn't be so hands-on any more, which was sad, and I missed our little chats over the fence as well. Howard also felt he was missing out but it was the right decision, we knew that. Jane said she was going to start teaching Dream some manners – things like walking obediently by your side, allowing his feet to be handled and climbing up a horsebox ramp – so when he did move to a proper trainer he'd be ready. It was the next stage in the plan. We had to just get used to it.

Dream was over there about six or seven months, but then we got a call from Christopher. His mares were all coming into season and what with Dream being 'entire' down below, he was concerned it might lead to difficulties.

For selfish reasons we decided we'd like Dream closer to home again so Howard found somewhere not too far from us. It didn't work out. Somehow Dream caught ringworm a couple of times, acquired a few mysterious knocks and had to go to the vets when another horse kicked him.

'This was a mistake,' Howard said. 'We need to get him out.'

Meanwhile, it was time to be thinking about stage two of the plan – getting the horse trained properly. Howard tracked down a contact number for Roger Charlton, a very prestigious flat trainer. He left various messages without much luck. Anxious to get Dream rehoused as quickly as possible, I got Roger's number off Howard and rang him up. It must have been my lucky day because he answered personally. He was out on the gallops, which is exactly where you'd want your expert to be, but it did mean there was a load of wind swirling down the phone making it very hard to hear.

'Look, Mr Charlton,' I shouted down the phone, 'I'm awful sorry to bother you, I don't mean to embarrass you with something that will never be the Rock of Gibraltar, but would you please come and have a look at our horse? We want your honest opinion before we spend silly money on training.'

For some reason he agreed. He went along one morning and phoned Howard back with his report. 'He's a nice-looking horse, without doubt. He won't be a flat racer, that's a guarantee, but there's something there. First things first: you need to have him gelded, put him away for another eighteen months, and then bring him out and see what you've got.'

Flat racers can start at two years old. Jumps horses have to wait till they're three and fully formed.

That was good enough for us. We brought Dream straight home to the allotment, Ron the vet did the necessary and then in September 2002, with Dream now eighteen months old, we drove back over the other side of Hereford to a place highly recommended. Chris Nebercheck had been a jockey in a former life so he had that knowledge as well. His partner did a lot of the work with the horses so she'd be the one to pick up teaching Dream his manners, getting him lunging and stretching as he ran; ready for proper training later. You can't do too much at that age because they're still growing. That's why you're not allowed to race until they're three (at least three on paper). I felt very happy leaving Dream there, although I was bemused that Chris never called him by his name. I'd go and visit most weekends and if Chris was around he'd say, 'Oh, you've come to see Ben, have you?' You had Brian calling him Ianto, the Syndicate calling him Dream, and now Chris was calling him Ben. If that horse grew up with split personalities I couldn't have blamed him.

Thanks to Roger Charlton, we now had a roadmap of what to do next. Howard was still our expert though. Over the next year and a bit, Howard began the search for the best possible trainer. There was no hurry due to the horse's age but he wanted to get it done. Then, at our regular catch-up in March 2004, he shared his findings. 'We need to forget about budget here,' he said. 'A good trainer can turn an average horse into a superstar.' I had to bow to his superior knowledge on that. I was also impressed when he said that now was the perfect time to get it sorted. March meant the sport was nearing the end of the jump season so all the trainers would just be coming out of their busiest times. 'They're much more likely to take on new business right now,' he said.

Off the top of his head Howard knew all the names of the good trainers, all their histories, and had come up with a shortlist.

'There are plenty of others,' he said, 'but there's no harm starting at the top.'

Between us we wrote to each name on his hit list. There was only one who didn't take the time to reply. Perhaps it got lost in the post. Everyone else either sent us a courteous rejection or said they'd take a look. That was all we could ask for.

Our top two choices were Nigel Twiston-Davies and Philip Hobbs. I'd never heard of either but apparently they were the bee's knees. As a racing fan Howard was pretty keen to meet Nigel Twiston-Davies, so he volunteered to visit that yard and Brian and I took the other one.

I phoned up, we made an appointment to go and then off we went. Sandhill Racing Stables is based in Minehead so it was a lovely drive along the coast to get there. One of the syndicate, Maldwyn Thomas, came along with us. It was a bit of an eye-opener for him, seeing the work Howard and I were doing behind the scenes.

We pulled into the yard. It looked like a working farm. It was nothing fancy, which told me the money was being spent in the right areas – namely on the horses. A good sign.

As we got out of the car one of the stable lasses was walking by.

'Excuse me, love,' Brian said, 'is the governor about?'

'Oh yes, he's in the house. Would you like me to get him?'

'If you wouldn't mind. Tell him I'm here about the jockey's job.'

Brian had a belly on him, he needed two sticks to walk and he was a bit out of breath from the effort of climbing out of a car.

The look on that poor girl's face! She stared at him for ages, transfixed I think, until Brian burst out laughing. It broke the ice, no question.

Philip Hobbs wasn't around but we met his number two, Johnson White. Now there's a man made for television. The way he carries himself, the way he speaks. He's an impressive man – but I don't think he was that taken with us at first. He admitted later that when he looked out the window he thought we were a bunch of holiday-makers escaped from the Butlin's camp up the road. I said, 'Oi, don't judge a book by its cover. We had an appointment you cheeky so and so.'

He might not be able to judge people, but that man's knowledge of horses is only beaten by his passion for them. It was obvious in everything he said and did. That's why he was happy based at the stables, working with the animals, while the boss was the public face at the races.

We got the full tour. There was nothing over the top, just everything where it should be and doing what it was made for, not just for show. There was a swimming pool, there were turfed gallops, there was woodchip, there was sand – you name it, they had it. Facilities aside, the real proof was in the horses. They all looked amazing. None of them were weaving or box walking. Far from looking stressed they appeared very happy and well-behaved. Whatever Sandhill did to them was working.

On top of it all, it was by the sea. Not only were the views from the gallops spectacular but going in the water every now and then was part of the training.

I said to Brian, 'If I were a horse, I'd love to live here.'

He said, 'I'd love to live here as I am! It's like a hotel on the bloody Riviera.'

So, we were sold. The only question now was: did they want *us*?

We left pictures of and documents for Dream Alliance and Johnson said they'd be in touch when he and Philip had had a chance to go through everything. Until then it was just a question of waiting.

'Well, that's sorted,' I said when we got back in the car. 'He's coming here.'

'What if Howard prefers this Twiston-Davies fella?' Maldwyn said.

'Then he'll be disappointed, won't he?'

I'm all bluster. If Howard had felt as strongly about the other place as I did about Philip then I'd have gone to visit it. In the event, he made an appointment to see Sand-hill and came away gushing like we did. Sometimes you just find the perfect fit for you and Philip Hobbs' set-up seemed tailor-made for us.

The syndicate took our word that this was the best option. There was no vote. It was in the constitution that certain decisions would be made by me and Howard. People didn't really mind. I think Maldwyn was the only syndicate member who made any visits when we were choosing. In the main, they trusted us to get the nuts and bolts right but if there had been an objection of course we'd have listened.

A day or so later we got the call from Philip himself to say Dream could go down to Minehead. There was no contract, no guarantee of them taking him on. 'We'll assess him, top to bottom, and if we see something we like, something we can work with, we'll find him a home. But I promise you this: if I don't think he can cut it I won't take your money and pretend he can.'

You couldn't say fairer than that. Arrangements for the handover were made. I wasn't part of it, which felt odd. Philip and his people were due to be at Cheltenham for the meeting after the festival so Chris Nebercheck drove Dream down there and left him with Philip. After that it was just more waiting.

Cefn Fforest in March isn't the sunniest of places so I bet my horse was enjoying better weather down in Minehead. As the days passed I became like Jekyll and Hyde. One minute I was anguishing that they didn't like my horse. The next I'd be saying to anyone who'd listen, 'Of course they'll accept him. I bred him myself.' It just depended when you caught me which version you got.

About a fortnight later, in early April, Philip rang. He's a quiet man, really, rather reserved. He doesn't enjoy the spotlight but he can talk horses until dawn.

'Now, your horse: he's willing, he wants to learn, he's doing everything we asked of him and at this stage that's all we need. He's not the fastest horse on the block and for that reason I don't think he will ever be a flat race runner' – exactly what Roger Charlton had said – 'but there's definitely enough there for us to work with. So with your permission we would like to keep him and see what we can do with him.'

I was so proud. Our working-class allotment boy being accepted by Philip was like Brian getting into Eton.

In April 2004 Howard called a syndicate meeting. He updated everyone on Dream's move to Minehead and explained how they were all welcome to visit. The only caveat was that they had to arrange any trips through him. The last thing Philip wanted was twenty-odd different people phoning him at all hours.

Ever a step ahead, Howard said to me afterwards, 'We need to be prepared for the next phase.'

'What's that?'

'For racing.'

He could barely stop himself from grinning as he said it. He really was making up for his lost youth.

'We need to think about the silks,' he said. 'What colours do you want Dream to run in?'

In horse racing, the jockey's outfit – or 'silks' as they are known – is designed by the horse's owners. Whether you have one entry in a race or five, all your jockeys will wear your colours. That has to be a nightmare for commentators. We only had the one horse so it seemed even more important to get it right.

'Oh, I hadn't given it any thought,' I said. 'I imagined you'd throw it open to the syndicate.'

'If we ask twenty people we'll get twenty different combinations. You're the breeder, why don't you pick the colours?'

I was touched by his offer. But I said, 'You don't think we're tempting fate now, do you? I don't want to jinx anything.'

'You're not having any doubts are you, Janet?'

I think he was almost pleased to see a crack in my armour.

'Give over, I just don't want to seem cocky. But I'll have a think.'

The combination I came up with was gunmetal grey and maroon. In my mind I saw this beautiful solid maroon tunic with grey epaulettes and armlets, and a grey cap with striking maroon and grey circles. Howard got the paperwork from Weatherbys, the body in charge of all colours in the sport, and filled it in. Once they checked that our combination and patterns weren't already in use, they sent the okay and Howard passed it over to Philip, who had better connections in the silks business than we did – i.e., he could get a better price – and the uniforms were made.

The whole process takes a while so I was glad Howard started it when he did. I soon forgot about it though. Then I was down at Sandhill one day visiting our boy when one of the stable lasses said, 'Your silks have arrived. Would you like to see them?'

'Oh, that would be lovely.'

She got the box and I tore it open like a kid at Christmas. I couldn't have been more disappointed.

Howard had put the colours the other way round, hadn't he!

Instead of a block of maroon we had a block of grey. At least the cap looked virtually as I wanted. I couldn't have a go at him, though, he'd done exactly what he thought I'd wanted. He just got it round his neck, that's all.

Ironically, I grew to love it and at the next syndicate meeting when a few people commented that it was a bit drab, I was its staunchest defender. It wasn't flashy or brash, it was serious with a dash of magic. Just like us.

My visits down to Philip's were pretty regular. Sometimes we'd get there early to watch Dream perform on the gallops. Sometimes we'd arrive when I knew he'd be in his stable. That was okay. I'd give him a cuddle and tell him about my week. If I had anything on my mind I'd let it out and always feel better afterwards. He was a wonderful listener. My rock, I would say, in many ways.

But he wasn't there just to help me. His training was coming along fine, Johnson said, and it was only a matter of time before we took the next step.

Sure enough, at the end of October 2004, six months after they'd taken him in, Philip rang Howard to say, 'I think it's time we saw what Dream can do. I'm going to enter him at Newbury next month.'

I wish I'd been there to see Howard's face. By the time he rang me Howard must have calmed down a bit but he was still excitable as a puppy. I have to admit I wasn't far behind.

'Oh, Howard,' I said, 'this is it, the dream is coming true.'

And I wasn't joking. It didn't matter what happened in

the race itself. The second Dream Alliance set off from the line he'd stop being a pet or a plaything or my cuddly toy and become something else. Something I'd dreamed of for six years.

A racehorse.

9

I Am *a Bloody Owner*

You'd have thought the Queen was coming to town. Everywhere I went – in Cfen Fforest, Blackwood, all over – people were stopping me and asking, 'Is your boy going to win?' I said the same thing to everyone: 'It's early days yet, he's finding his feet, I'll just be happy if he gets round in one piece.'

But I was lying. I didn't want to put pressure on him but I had the deluded confidence of any proud mother. He wasn't just going to get round, he was going to make a name for himself. I knew it. *He won't let us down*, I thought. *Not my Dream.*

Philip Hobbs was as measured as ever. He said, 'You can do whatever you like with them at home but until they actually get into a race with all the other horses you don't know what they are going to do. He will be green but I predict he will have a go. If he comes tenth he'll be showing the level of progress we expect. Anything less than that and we might have to reconsider his potential.'

'In other words,' Howard said, 'reading between the lines, he's saying eleventh or below and we'd need to find a new trainer.'

I took an even darker message from it.

'I think actually it's worse than that, Howard. Eleventh or below and he's saying we'd better get another hobby. Luckily he's not going to let us down.'

Howard reported the conversation with Philip back to the syndicate. Some people said Philip was joking. Some said he was lying. Some said he was plain wrong. In other words, everyone thought Dream stood a chance – just like I did. That's the blinkers of parenthood again for you, right there.

The optimists extended outside the syndicate. I'd never bet on a horse in my life but my mother said one day, 'Are you going to back your boy?'

'I don't know,' I said, 'I don't even buy a lottery ticket. I'll ask Brian.'

'Well, if you do have a wager, I'll go in with you.'

I did indeed approach my husband and he said, 'Of course I'm having a bet. This is our boy out there. We've got to show him support.'

In the end I got a tenner from Brian, a tenner from my mother, a tenner from my daughter Sasha and I added a tenner myself. Brian then placed that £40 on Dream Alliance each way. In other words, he didn't need to win. As long as he was 'placed' – that is to say, as long as he came in the top five, depending on the amount of runners – we would be in the money. Not as much money as if we just bet all out on the win, but enough to make it worthwhile.

I have to be honest. Come the day of the race, not one of us expected to see a penny of that cash again.

I never liked flat racing. When I was concocting my masterplan it was the hurdles and fences I envisaged my as-yet-unborn horse tackling, not running up and down an elongated golf course. Where's the challenge in that? I was no expert on racing but when I thought of horses it was National Hunt racing that I always imagined. What's more beautiful than watching the sinews rippling as a horse leaps over a wall or a bush or some other hurdle? Brian used to watch the racing while I was cooking and usually I had no interest in it, but every so often I'd look over and there'd be a slow motion shot of a horse just about clearing the hedge and you could make out every single moving part of his legs and his shoulders and his neck. It was awesome and I think that's what I was imagining when I got this bee in my bonnet. Horses jumping and looking amazing doing it; it wasn't much more complicated than that.

Not everyone agrees of course. You ask some people what event defines horse racing for them and they'll say the Derby. Her Majesty, I hear, would be one of them. I wouldn't criticize anyone for their opinion, of course, especially not Her Majesty, but obviously they are wrong (sorry, Ma'am). The pinnacle of racing is the Grand National every day of the week, shortly followed by the Scottish, Irish and, of course, the Welsh versions of that esteemed event. Win one of those, the experts I spoke to all agreed, and you have a proper horse on your hands. We'd be heading to Newbury Race Course, just south of the M4 over in Berkshire. That place has got everything. It's equipped to host horses racing on the flat as well as over the jumps so it's open all year. Every expert we'd spoken to so far had said Dream was exactly what I wanted, a jumps racer, plain and simple. We knew he wouldn't have the speed to really compete on the flat but he had the heart and the personality to fight when he wanted to.

Which is why it was so discombobulating to find ourselves about to cheer on our lad in a race *on the flat*.

'Philip,' I said, 'are you sure about this? I thought you said he couldn't manage the flats?'

'You're right, that's exactly what I said. But all the horses in this race are jump novices. None of them have run before. You always start them off on the flat if you can, just to get them used to the pack and the whip.'

What did I know? The race Philip entered Dream for – the 'EBF/Lane Fox "Junior" Standard Open National Hunt Flat Race' to give it its full title, known to everyone else as 'the 4.05 at Newbury' – was, it turns out, designed specifically for horses like ours. In other words, horses aged three bred for the jumps, but just starting out. Before they risk the animals going hell for leather over fences, the governing body of the sport prefers you to have a go on the flat first, just to get them used to running in a pack, the blinkers, and the starting gun – the basics really. 'Bumper' races they call these try-outs. Jump horses are allowed a maximum of four of these types of flat races. After that, it's the big boys waiting.

If they don't make complete fools of themselves first.

I was like a child waiting for Christmas. Every night it was getting harder and harder to sleep I was that excited. Our race was 10 November 2004. On the ninth of the month I was super confident. Same on the eighth, seventh, sixth – in fact, every day since Philip announced he'd entered it. Even waking up that Wednesday morning I was bouncing around the house like Tigger, chatting nineteen to the dozen, probably to hide my nerves. And then something changed. I came over all sick, nauseous.

Oh my god, I'm going to be too ill to travel.

I took myself into the bathroom. I was looking in the mirror when I realized there was nothing physically wrong with me. I was just worried. Worried about Dream's first race. Worried that he wouldn't perform.

Worried that I'd look a complete prat.

It was horrible, it was. This massive cloud was hanging over me. There were voices in my head saying, 'What do you know about racing? Who do you think you are taking on proper owners? You think you know more than the sheikhs of this world? This horse of yours, it comes from a slag heap, doesn't it? What's he going to achieve?'

I thought I was going mad. I'm such a positive person normally, yet my own brain was telling me I was going to fail. The humiliation if that happened. I'd had the entire village patting me on the back for days and we hadn't even run a step yet. Complete strangers were pinning their hopes on this horse they'd never heard of, bred by a woman they only knew by name. And as for the syndicate. These people – good, honest people – had answered the call in my hour of need and invested in the dream that I had sold them. The 'Dream' that was racing today. What if I'd got it wrong? These weren't millionaire investors. Some of them couldn't spare ten pound a week without cutting back on essentials. What if I'd wasted their money?

I'd invested God knows what of my own money as well, with and without Brian's knowledge. Worse than that, I had given everyone hope. That's a very hard thing to pay back if it is taken away.

And as for Howard, losing his youth would be the least of his troubles if Dream Alliance didn't succeed. If he lost money on Dream Alliance because of me he might lose his marriage and all. Angela's a lovely lady but she'd been down that road before. Did I want all of that on my conscience?

I managed to calm down but the worry stayed there all morning in the back of my mind.

What if he turns out to be a donkey? What if I'm a laughing stock?

With Newbury on the M4 you can imagine how many Welsh people turn up there regularly. This particular Wednesday there were thirty-odd more. Sadly, not everyone in the syndicate was in work so they had the time. Even those that did have a nine to five made their excuses and headed down, most of them with their husbands and wives. A load of the lads got a minibus and travelled down together. Alcohol was enjoyed, I believe. It was that kind of day.

Brian and I drove down with Sasha. We didn't go direct. En route we stopped at the cemetery to lay flowers on the graves of Brian's parents. We were frequent visitors but on this day he wanted their help. If they weren't busy and they had the time and inclination, he'd like them to keep an eye on our horse. It sounds silly maybe, a bit pagan perhaps, but it felt right at the time.

From the cemetery the conversation in the car became tense. Brian, as he always does, tried to keep the tone light but I only had monosyllabic answers which, if you know me at all, is very, very unusual. I was a bag of nerves and I couldn't shake it.

As we got close to the course the phone messages were pinging around. 'Where are you?'

'How far away are you?'

'We're here. What are you doing?'

'Which entrance is it?'

'I'm lost – help me!'

We had everything. People were buzzing and giddy with excitement. No one apart from Howard had ever done anything like this before. Even he was quivering in his boots with anticipation. The whole day just felt so special for so many people. And, to a large extent, I was responsible for that. Brian told me as much. Howard said the same before we set off.

'None of us would be going anywhere if it weren't for you, Janet. Thank you for that. Thank you for everything.'

It was nice to hear but did it help my nerves?

Did it heck.

I'd never set foot on a racecourse before. I'd never even been in a bookies. According to my font of racing knowledge, Newbury is one of the more elite tracks. They get a better type of horse there and, with it, generally, a better – by which they mean 'richer' – type of owner.

Well, I thought, *they're in for a shock today.*

We weren't the first to arrive, not by a long shot. The lads' bus had been there since opening. They wanted every second of their jolly to count. I got the feeling that the day out was as important as their horse being involved. Even that, Brian said, was a positive.

'You've done that, you have. Whatever happens, those

lads are going to have the day of their lives because of you.'

For some of them it was almost over before it began. At the course there was an entrance for punters and another one for trainers and owners. The last time I saw him, Tony Kerby said, 'I'm not being ripped off paying £6 for a burger down there – I'll be taking my sandwiches.' Logical, good common sense, classic Tony. But picture the scene: he arrives at the correct entrance alongside all the toffs and the obvious moneyed people and the security guards take one look at this lad jogging up with his carrier bag and say, 'Excuse me, mate, you need the other entrance over the way.'

'I don't think I do,' Tony says.

'Sir, this is the entrance for trainers and owners.'

'I *am* a bloody owner!'

Of course, they apologized and let him in because he had the right ticket. Double checking most likely. Not that I was thinking about that. I was still wracked with the fear that everything was going to come crashing down.

Stepping through the door into the owners' enclosure for the first time is magical. You're so close to the track. The colours are striking. There's green as far as you can see. Above it, the clear, bright blue expanse of the crisp winter sky. Behind us the white lines of the grandstands populated by dots of faces and hats and jackets. And to the left and the right around us, the pinks and the reds and the blacks of all the owners' outfits. It wasn't Ascot posh, it wasn't top hats and tails, but it was smart – at a minimum the men had to wear a collared shirt, for example – and it smelled expensive. There was a rarefied, almost sanctified feel to the area, no mistake. And we were part of it.

When you've got the golden ticket we had you can go anywhere in the course. Punters are kept corralled up in their grandstands but we could go down by the rail, or stay in our own private enclosure, anywhere we wanted. For a few of the lads and lasses with us, that was Mecca. If you're a gambler you want to be as close to the horses as possible and with our passes you could do that. You could get right up close as they came out to parade, take a look at them and get your bet on quick.

One of the other perks of being an owner is you get a free programme. I've still got mine. It says on the front: 'complimentary – not for resale'. The people in the cheap seats had to pay £2 so I was winning before the first race started.

Flicking through to our race I was all fingers and thumbs. But there it was, the seventh race of the day, the 4.05, and there in black and white at number eight was our boy: Dream Alliance. Seeing our horse in the programme made everything feel real. Our jockey for the day was Paul Flynn, one of the riders attached to Philip's stable.

If I'd felt apprehensive before, I had the weight of the world on my shoulders now. The only good news was that there appeared to be only eleven runners. If Dream came tenth it wasn't so bad. Then I turned the page . . . in total there were twenty-three horses running. For some of them, like us, it was their debut. For others it could have been their third or fourth race. Suddenly getting tenth seemed a lot harder.

Especially when Howard said, 'Have you seen who's riding number one?'

The first horse listed, 'Bayside', had a pedigree to make you green with envy. But it was the jockey, A. P. McCoy, that had Howard twitching. I'd never heard of him. The only horse rider I really knew was Princess Anne. 'That man has been the champion jockey every year since he started,' Howard said. 'We're up against the top dogs here.'

A. P. McCoy would go on to become the single most successful jockey in history. He was awarded Champion Jockey at the National Hunt in every single one of the twenty years he raced. But if you don't know someone's reputation you can't be scared of it, can you? Sometimes ignorance really is bliss.

Something in the programme that didn't affect us was the prize money. There was a decent purse for such a low-calibre race. The winner was down to get £2,103, second place £683 and third £342. I didn't read much further than that but something that did catch my eye was an extra reward of £750 to the breeder of the winning horse. That was interesting. I never knew there was a separate prize for that. Not that it would ever come to it, I supposed, but I thought, *Lucky that I am our registered breeder.*

Throughout the day, little groups from the syndicate drifted off, moved apart, mingled, stayed together, every which way you like. Some would go into one area to have something to eat and drink and others would mosey off elsewhere. As four o'clock approached we all congregated at the rail. It was slightly raised so you could see the course but you were also within touching distance of the parade ring. For everything else there was a big TV screen conveniently positioned so you didn't miss a second of the action. All the lads who had been drinking all day were shouting and pretty boisterous I'd have to say. You couldn't begrudge them. This was why they joined the syndicate, for days like this, to have a drink and a laugh and a bet or two among friends. For all the bravado at the meetings, for all the talk of winning, it turned out no one expected anything from our horse. The day out was a good enough excuse to be involved.

I'd like to say that made me feel better. It didn't. I wasn't in it for other people's praise. If Dream didn't perform it wouldn't matter what anyone said, I would take the shame to my grave.

As the start of the race approached my heart was

racing. Palpitations, sweating, lack of focus – you name it, I had it. I vaguely remember standing alongside Brian, Howard, Maureen Jones and Kevin French, but I wouldn't swear on it. I was in that much mental turmoil I didn't know what was going on.

We were all of us down by the rails, that much I remember. The parade ring was just to our right. One by one the horses began to emerge from behind the stands and the cheering started. Well, it did from us. Hardly any of the punters so much as looked up. The ones that did were just checking the horse they'd bet on had four legs. Then they went back to their beers. As for the other owners milling around us, they were more the champagne brigade but I can't say a drop was spilt in excitement. I got the distinct feeling they'd seen it all before.

But not us. We were on tenterhooks waiting for our boy to emerge and, oh, the noise when he did . . .

Maldwyn was the first to shout out: 'There he is, there he is, number eight!'

There was such a roar you'd think we were cheering him home across the finish line.

'Over there, number eight,' someone said.

'That one, with the rider in grey.'

I didn't need a number to recognize my boy. There could have been a hundred there, all chestnut with a white blaze on their heads and I'd have spotted him. Paul Flynn looked fantastic on top. I was so proud seeing him wear the silks I'd designed. Of course, it didn't take long for one or two naysayers to emerge from the group.

'Is that it?' one of them said. 'It's a bit boring, isn't it, all that grey?'

They weren't specifically addressing me, but they were saying it within my earshot. It was the booze talking, I suppose. I could have bitten my tongue. I could have blamed Howard and said he'd got it wrong, but I preferred to suggest that maybe any negativity could be kept until after the race. Or, preferably, never. 'If you think you could do better then perhaps you should get more involved,' I said. 'I didn't see any of you giving up your evening to fill in the paperwork.'

I think it was the stress of the day making me speak out.

Someone promptly changed the subject, there was more drunken laughter and we moved on. It would have been a shame to spoil a momentous day. But honestly, there's a time and a place for criticism. When your horse is about to make its debut, that's neither.

I was disappointed I couldn't go over and give Dream a hug. Even so, as far away as I was, I looked into that horse's deep brown eyes and I said to him, 'I haven't forgotten my promise. Whether this is your first of many races or your first and last, do your best, my love, give me everything and when it's all over you're coming home to the allotment and your mother with me.'

Whether he heard me or not I can't say, but it felt important that I said it aloud.

That sickness I'd felt in the morning was back with dividends. I had so much riding on this race personally – not including our each-way bet – I was determined not to miss a second. I watched as the horses gathered by the line. There are no gates, the jockeys line them up as best they can. There was bobbing and manoeuvring, a moment of stillness and then the crack of the starting pistol. That was the last thing I saw.

I tore away from the rail and started pacing up and down. If a horse did this in his box they'd think he was troubled. Maybe I was. All I can say for sure is I could not watch that race. I don't know why. But the second Dream took off I knew I couldn't bear to see him fail. Or worse.

It hadn't occurred to me before, but what if he fell? You know what they do to injured horses, and it's not a plaster and lollipop.

Oh my god, what have I got him into?

Although I couldn't see, the commentary from the loudspeakers was impossible to ignore. The names at the front kept changing. At the first mention of Dream Alliance there was a massive cheer from our group and frankly it never stopped. They kept it up, yelling and screaming for our boy. I heard one bloke have a go, saying, 'It's not a football match you know.' I don't know who spoke back to him but he did keep quiet after that.

If you're young or European, the race was 2,500 metres. If you're slightly older or a horse aficionado, it was one mile and four-and-a-half furlongs. It wasn't going to take much more than a few minutes but, my God, it felt like an eternity. The commentator was going on and on about High Altitude, Floragalore, Inaro, Bully-rag and Cousin Nicky. There was the odd mention of Bayside and young Tom Scudamore's Classic Quart but the rest of the pack were out in the cold. Right until the end, that is.

From where the lads of our group were standing, the finishing straight was in sight. Regardless of whatever the commentator was saying, it was the distinctive and very deafening roars coming from my friends that I was focusing on. They were screaming, they were shouting, they were out of their minds with excitement.

What was happening? Where was he? I had to know.

But I still couldn't look.

It was over as suddenly as it was started. The majority of the grandstands came to a still silence. Behind me my friends calmed down considerably. They were listening. We were all listening as the commentator called the result. His voice was so high-pitched he sounded like he was on helium.

'First,' he squeaked, 'Inaro; second, High Altitude;

third, Cousin Nicky. And fourth, making his debut, is number eight, Dream Alliance.'

Oh. You. Little. Beauty.

I knew you wouldn't let me down . . .

10

Ask Him Yourself

I swear all you could hear then was Welsh accents.

Not that you could make out what was being said. We were screaming, we were shouting, we were whooping. You know when you see a dog or a toddler so excited they don't know how to express it, so they just run around like a headless chicken? That was us. Thirty adults all behaving like children who've overdosed on Sunny D. Fabulous it was.

I don't think Philip knew what had hit him. Most of the syndicate he'd never seen before so when Howard introduced him to the gang he got mobbed. He's not the most gregarious of characters and to be honest he seemed a bit embarrassed by the attention. Scared even. He looked like a rabbit in the headlights. But people just wanted, correctly, to thank him for producing such a good performance. He wouldn't hear of it. That's what he's like. For Philip it's all about the horse.

'Don't thank me,' he managed to say above the din. 'It's Dream Alliance who did all the work.'

When I got Philip alone by the rail he was a bit more relaxed and businesslike. More like the Philip I knew.

'Your boy did well,' he said. 'I knew he had it in him but until you see them in a race you never really know for sure. Some of the best horses I've seen have frozen when it comes to the main event. Your Dream, I can say with confidence, is not one of those. He's a fighter. He wants to run and he wants to please. We can go places with this one.'

'Can we get to over there?' I said, pointing to the winners' enclosure where the place horses – that is to say, the top three – and their jockeys were being congratulated by delirious owners. There was even a little trophy being handed out. I'm not usually one to crave what someone else has. We all make our luck. But I liked the look of being over there, of being noticed.

'I'm not one to make promises,' Philip said, 'you know that, but I don't see why not. There's a lot of work to do but if things go as I anticipate then yes, you should be experiencing that enclosure before long.'

'Thank you,' I said, 'thank you for everything.'

I think I just wanted to see him look embarrassed again.

Philip made his escape and I stood and watched as Dream milled around with the other non-winners in their area over the way. There didn't seem to be much going on so I dug out my phone and rang my father. He was terminally housebound through illness, sadly, but desperate to keep up with Dream's progress. I'd promised to phone the minute I knew. In all the jubilation I was running a bit late.

He was so happy for me but not as delighted as Mum. When she prised the phone out of Dad's hands it was mainly to see how her bet had done. If it weren't for the fact she wasn't in the best of health either I think there could have been cartwheels.

'Don't you be so late in phoning me next time,' my father said. 'I don't want to find everything out from the newspapers.'

I promised I'd be more prompt in future and I stuck to it. For the rest of his life I would call him directly after a race finished. Win, lose or stumble, he was always over the moon to get the call.

As I was chatting I was vaguely aware of things happening to the horses. They were gathering in a sort of line. As soon as I hung up I turned to my racing encyclopaedia and dragged Howard away from the melée. 'What's going on with our boy?' I asked him.

'It's just procedure,' he said. 'They have to be weighed along with their jockeys to make sure no one is travelling light.'

For our race every horse had to be carrying a weight of ten stone twelve pounds. That was fixed. If you had a jockey who weighed exactly that then great in theory, except his saddle would take him over so the horse would have to carry more. If you had a jockey so small he barely moved the scales then the groom would put weights in the saddle to bring the balance up. Ideally you wanted a jockey and his saddle to naturally make the weight.

Before the race the jockey is weighed and the horse furniture is weighed. Then, just to make sure there's been no skulduggery, it's all done again after. And that's what we were waiting for.

'What happens if someone's under?' I asked.

'Then they'll promote all the other runners up one position.'

'Oh,' I said, 'so we could still come third?'

'In theory we could win it but it rarely happens. They're just making sure.'

I could see Dream milling around the parade ring with the others. I was so proud of him. But, like Philip, I knew he had more. Was it my imagination or was he looking over at the winners' enclosure?

'That's right,' I said to myself, 'you look over there. That's your rightful home, that is. That's where you belong.'

For a lot of the lads, the day out was the reason for getting involved in the syndicate. It was sociable, it was fun and it made them a bit of money. They'd be betting on the races anyway, some of them, so why not do it at the racetrack rather than in some grim bookies?

One by one they all made their way over to me to

Me aged five at our 141 Commercial Street flat with my mother in the background.

Brian, aged twenty-one, while we were courting. This was one of his projects!

Our wedding day in October 1971. I borrowed my dress and veil from one of my work colleagues.

Top to bottom:

Me, aged eighteen, with my cousin and my grandad, who is holding Dennis.

Another one of Brian's horses. You can see his old cart in the background.

With the very handsome Rags To Riches (Charlie) after winning best of breed.

Top to bottom:

Saying hello to one of our pigeons.

Just some of the trophies we won with the birds.

Brian and I in the 80s on one of our caravan holidays.

Top to bottom:

The Top Club in Cefn Fforest
where I was working when I
came up with the idea to breed
a race horse.

Dream's father Bien Bien who
was a Champion Turf Horse
in the USA.

Dream as a foal with Rewbell
and Brian.

Top to bottom:

Our allotment where
Dream was raised. The
stable is on the left.

Brian sharing a moment
with Dream (aged
eighteen months).

Recurring Dream training
at Sandhill Racing Stables
with Philip Hobbs.

Ianto on our allotment with Brian. We brought him up together after Rewbell's death.

Tom O'Brien riding Dream to victory in the Coral Welsh National in 2009.

A delighted Tom following his win – I'd had every faith in him!

The syndicate celebrating with Dream in the winner's enclosure. We were all so proud.

Dream at the Aintree Grand National in 2010. It wasn't his race and he pulled up at the twenty-fourth fence.

Enjoying a day out at Aintree! *From left to right:*
Brian, me, Angela and Howard.

thank me for giving them something extra. I felt like Father Christmas. All these people grateful because of something I'd given them. There wasn't a negative voice to be heard. Not quite, anyway. Howard's brother Gwyn, who'd come along to support his brother and, to be fair, had had a few glasses already, found me by the rails and didn't look happy.

'Well, thank you very much, Janet,' he said, 'for ruining a perfectly good day out.'

'I beg your pardon?'

'I thought this was just going to be a laugh. I thought we were just here for the beer and the bets. I didn't realize we had a potential winner on our hands. I suppose we'll have to take it more seriously now!'

Then he gave me a great big bear hug and raised his glass.

'You've done a wonderful thing for everyone here. I want you to know that.'

I wish I could have bottled that moment. Even just recorded it. Some of the things that happened later would make me question whether it really happened . . .

We were the last race of the day, so the stands started emptying shortly after. Not that we noticed. Fourth might not sound much to any of the millionaire owners, but for his first time out, a little horse bred by a woman who'd not worked with anything larger than a whippet, and raised on an allotment standing on the site of an old slag heap, it was a miracle.

And it won us some dosh.

Because there were so many riders the payouts went all the way down to fourth and fifth. I don't understand the mathematics but a £40 each-way bet at 7/1 produced winnings of £48. Brian's little face when he came back from the bookies was a picture.

Something else Philip said when the carnival had calmed down was that the Newbury course had been too short for Dream. 'He was going strong at the end. Very strong. I think over a longer course he could have done better.'

So a plan was hatched. His next race would be longer. Two miles, something like that. Philip would have a look and see what was out there in the next month or two. It would have to be another bumper race but the trainer wanted a strong field. There's no point conning ourselves we're better than we are by running with donkeys. Dream had proved he wasn't afraid of the environment or the challenges. 'Let's get him working as soon as possible,' Philip said.

Unfortunately, it didn't happen. We were going about our business, trying to live our daily lives as though this magical thing hadn't happened, when Howard got a call from Sandhill. He rang me and said, 'Dream's tweaked something on the gallops this morning. He's not going to be running again this month.'

'Poor love,' I said, 'I'll have a look when I'm down at the weekend.'

When I got there Dream's eyes were as bright as ever so the spirit was there. But his rear left leg was strapped. Johnson said something had gone, a pulled muscle probably, but it wasn't anything to worry about. 'It happens to young horses. There's no permanent damage but no cure either. We just have to wait until it heals.'

Whether he knew how long it would take I don't know but November came and went, Christmas flew by and the New Year looked like it wasn't hanging around either. We got to March 2005 and I said, as I did every week, 'Is there any progress?'

'It's healing, we're sure of that. We can tell by the way he's walking. But even if he runs in the next week or two it's going to take time to get his strength back up. You can't rush these things. If we do he'll pay for it later.'

Summer was upon us before we blinked. I can't say much happened except every week or so Brian and I would drive over to Minehead and see our boy. It's a different dynamic when you're not expecting anything. You're not there to watch him train. You just want to help him get better. So I'd go in the stable, have a chat with him, tell him my news and he'd look at me with those great dark pools of eyes and I'd know he was listening.

It's funny. I told that horse things that I'd never told Brian or my mother or my best friends. He never judged. He just listened and let me rattle on and on. I like to think I was as good a friend. Really, though, he should have had a few more. Every time I saw one of the syndicate they'd badger me about when he was going to race.

'Ask him yourself next time you're down there,' I'd say, knowing virtually none of them ever visited, so that shut them up. Until the next time and it would happen all over again.

I wasn't worried about Dream getting back to racing. In his first outing he'd achieved what I'd set out to do. He'd come fourth in a serious race beating some better horses carrying some much more experienced riders. If he never ran competitively again I'd have ticked that box. What's more, if it was over, he'd soon be coming home with me. Either way, personally, it was win-win.

But for his own sake I wanted Dream to be healthy. I wanted him to get strong again and prove himself. No one really knows what horses have in their locker and no one really knows what they're thinking, but Philip and Johnson swore that some horses only came alive during a race. They'd had some very good runners who'd won everything but never seemed to enjoy it. Then there were the others who just got on with their lives, looked nothing special, but you showed them a race and they grew and grew. That was their stage. That was where they belonged. That was what they lived for.

Dream, they both said, fell into that camp. If he never raced again it would be a tragedy for him personally. He needed it, he thrived on it. It was in his DNA. The rest of his life, like most horses, you could boil down to just chewing carrots and pooing. Dream was destined for so much more.

But first he had to get well.

The buzz in Cefn Fforest and its outlying areas was radio-active after Dream's first race. I can't say I know everyone in the village but most of them seemed to know me. The working men's club in particular had a bit of a party feel the weekend after the race. A lot of the syndicate came along for the night as well. The sense of jubilation we'd felt at Newbury continued there.

Plenty of drinkers in the bar admitted they hadn't thought Dream had had a chance.

'No offence, Janet, but you've got to admit you've done something out of the ordinary there.'

'Say what you like but we only did what I said we'd do. You wanna listen next time.'

'Well I'll be having a bet next time, don't you worry.'

Some people wanted to get even more involved. One guy said, 'I'd like a piece of your syndicate, Janet. How do I go about it?'

I said, 'You'll have to ask Howard Davies. But I don't see why not.'

Actually, Howard was very keen. He knew where everything was money-wise and to be on top of Dream's finances going forward we ideally needed another three or four people. Because of the way the syndicate was organized, though, with everyone paying monthly and then taking a slice of Dream's winnings at the end of his career, Howard couldn't just let newcomers join without catching up the payments.

'People don't like Johnny-come-latelys getting preferential treatment,' he said. 'Everyone else has put in £480. New members are welcome but they'll have to make up the difference. Otherwise it's not fair when we divide the winnings.'

'Come on, Howard, that's not reasonable. These are people without a penny to their name really. They don't have £480 to give you. They'll struggle with a tenner each week. You need to find another way.'

So we kicked it around and I managed to persuade him that we should freeze the £480. If people wanted to be part of Dream's journey but they didn't have the capital, they could start paying monthly and we'd say they owed £480. Then if the horse did make some money, when we had a share out they'd get their wedge less what they owed. It seemed straightforward enough to me.

At the end of the day, as far as Howard was concerned it was all about balancing the books. He still felt we should run it by the others. At the next meeting he proposed we let in new members and when it came to the share out they'd get theirs pro rata. In case anyone was wavering he also made the point that if we didn't get some additional members there might come a time when everyone else's subscriptions went up a notch. I'm not saying that swung the vote but we got the motion carried and within a month we were up to twenty-three full-time members: Paul Lavercombe, Mike Davey, Gordon Hogg, Pete Woodhall, Howard Davies, Brian Vokes, Kevin French, Maureen Jones, Tony Kerby, Susan Llandrygan, Christine Brunnock, Martin Thomas, Eddie Thomas, Lee Baldwyn, Stuart Lewis, Gerwyn Evans, Gareth Gwilt, Maldwyn Thomas, Ralph Howells, Eira Williams, Peter Bevan, Ray Gardner and David Potter.

All we needed now was a horse fit to race.

With some people you worry that they're just taking your money. Especially if they know you don't have the experience and you're relying on their expertise. Think about the last time you took a car into a garage. Whatever the grease monkey says you have to go along with. They know it and you know it, that's just the way it is. You might feel you're being ripped off but you don't have the know-how to prove it. That never for one second crossed my mind with Philip. He wasn't sitting on Dream for a year to mess with us. He had no shortage of people wanting their horses trained by him. It wasn't about the money. And his right hand man Johnson White couldn't have gone along with it anyway. He's a winner. He doesn't want old nags hanging around just to collect the rent. In short, the fact Dream was still there after eleven months meant they maintained their faith in him. Which meant we all did.

I was down at Philip's stable in October 2005 as I was

every week. To my eyes Dream was looking strong, eager even. He put up with my chat and still had some fire in his eyes. That was a good sign.

When Johnson came over he agreed. 'He's ready,' he said. 'I think Philip wants to enter him at Cheltenham.'

'What, in March?'

'No, in a fortnight.'

There weren't quite thirty of us heading down to Cheltenham on 26 October 2005, but still a sizeable number, what with the various syndicate members and their partners. Once again we stopped off at Brian's parents' graves to pay our respects and ask for any help they could give from their side. And once again my mother, daughter, husband and myself put on a bet. Even though he'd last run nearly a year earlier, the bookies had Dream as the favourite at 5/2. In other words, for every two pounds we put on, we'd get five back. That only mattered if we won so Brian stuck with the policy of an each-way wager. Any place down to five would pay out something.

The race was another flat organized by the National Hunt for its fledgling jumpers. There were seventeen runners and once again the fabled A. P. McCoy was among the jockeys, riding Kevkat at 9/2. He hadn't placed ahead of us at Newbury so I wasn't quaking in my boots this time. Howard was the nervous one. 'It's only a matter of time before he shows his class,' he insisted. 'You mark my words.'

Richard Johnson was our pilot this time. This was a bit of a coup, actually, as he was Philip's top man. He'd already won the Cheltenham Gold Cup, not for the last time, and would go on to become Champion Jockey (having been runner up to A. P. McCoy for sixteen years!). Even then we knew he had something about him.

The jockey wasn't the only change. The silks were different this time too, with the word 'Amlin' stitched on. Because the uniforms were technically part of his stable, Philip was allowed to sell sponsorship for the horse. He got a shilling or two from the equine insurance company he used to look after his business. It didn't trickle down to us unfortunately, but I have to say it looked professional having an advert on our silks.

Speaking of sponsorship, our race was officially called the Weatherbys Bank Standard Open National Hunt Flat Race Class H – but to us it was the 5.30 at Cheltenham. That's what you'd be betting on in the bookies.

The dark was descending long before the start. I had every intention of watching our boy but the second the starting pistol went off I turned away. Again. The long and the short of it was I couldn't bear to see Dream fail. I didn't think he would but horses always have it in them. They only need to hit a pothole, have a little stumble and they're over. Snap a bone and it could be fatal, depending on what the course vet said. I couldn't bear it if that happened to him.

So I listened to the course commentator again instead.

I must have been the only person facing away from the track. But I drank in every word he said. From the off Nigel Twiston-Davies's Dopey Bob, ridden by Carl Llewellyn, was in contention. I kept hearing his name followed by Tokala from Brendan Powell's stable. A. P. McCoy's Kevkat was a constant as was El Bandindos and in the early stages Carrickerry. I didn't care about any of them. All I wanted to hear was the name 'Dream Alliance' and after a minute or so I did. He was in the pack for ages, chasing the leaders, sniffing around behind them, keeping steady as the pretenders fell away. As Tokala emerged as the leader to beat, Richard Johnson kept Dream steady while the others tired. Fifth, fourth, third – the momentum was the stuff of dreams. It was like watching Seb Coe devour the leaders in the Olympics. He was hoovering them up. I was so tempted to turn round and watch but I couldn't. I didn't dare.

In the final straight it came down to a battle between Tokala and Dream Alliance. I thought the commentator was going to explode it was so tense. The last half furlong was the stuff of legend. Dream pushed and pushed and pushed but so did another horse, Mr Nick. A lot of front runners would have buckled under the pressure. Tokala didn't and nabbed the win. I couldn't complain. After a layoff of eleven months Dream Alliance had marked his return to the sport with a second place. And beaten the so-called legend A. P. McCoy yet again.

I enjoyed phoning my father to tell him that.

The winner's enclosure at Cheltenham was packed to say the least. Every one of us went down there to cuddle Dream and have our pictures taken. For some of the syndicate it was the first time they'd touched their prize asset. It wasn't for me to judge but I didn't think I could have been involved with a horse without some kind of relationship. That's what I thought after, anyway. At that moment I wasn't thinking of them; if I'm honest, I wasn't thinking of anyone but myself. I just wanted to say two words to my boy.

'Thank you.'

I knew it was wrong but I took everything he did personally. When he came fourth at Newbury I was cock of the walk and so when he was sick for a year I had to take that on my shoulders as well. Coming second gave me such a thrill it was like I'd run the course myself. If my life ended at that moment I couldn't have complained about anything.

Not only did Brian pick up another batch of winnings on our behalf but there was also the matter of prize money to consider. First place in the 5.30 collected £3,672.30. Not a bad sum, if a little random. The pot for second was £1,130. The amount didn't matter. All I cared about was the name on the cheque: 'The Alliance Syndicate'.

Philip was happy of course. I had to say, 'You were right about the longer length.' Cheltenham was two miles and half a furlong, and whilst plenty of horses had led or challenged and dropped away, Dream had not showed any signs of tiring.

Philip added, 'I think your boy could have run all day. He has the heart, I've always said that. As long as he's in a marathon and not a sprint he will be there or thereabouts in the shakeup.'

More than the result, that was what I wanted to hear. If Philip thought Dream had a future then we were pointing in the right direction.

Of course, we were still only racing on the flat. The proof of the pudding would be in the jumps. When, I wanted to know, would that be?

'I think he's ready,' Philip said. 'Our next bumper will be the real deal. Let's see what the boy can really do, shall we?'

Horses are wonderful creatures. We'd geared everything up so Dream Alliance would be ready to take on the world – or fall flat on his face – as soon as he turned three. But after he'd pulled a muscle and was out for a year, we realized that his age didn't matter really. It was just us being impatient. If anything he was fitter, faster and stronger than a four-year-old. At least, that's the way he looked at Cheltenham. His third race would prove whether we had a flash in the pan or a proper hope. Anything above fifth Philip said would be a positive. It wasn't about the result, it was about the performance.

For our next outing it would be the same set-up: novice racers having a run-out before they launch themselves at the grown-up stuff. I think it was incredible anyone was interested. To me the races were little more than warm-ups. But where there's a field there's a market for the turf accountants and so our races were as prominent as anything else on the card each meeting.

Race number three in Dream's diary was on 14 December 2005. It was a return to Newbury but on a different course to the one he'd started at. Like Cheltenham, this was a shade over two miles – two furlongs and 183 yards over, to be precise. But this time there was a very obvious difference. In order to get round the course Dream would have to negotiate ten hurdles. His bumper days were over. This really was time to put up or shut up. Could he do it? Could he make a go of National Hunt?

When I first started, I thought racing was either flat or jumps. Howard educated me that jumps came in two categories. You had the hurdles or you had the steeplechase. In hurdles, the obstacles were a minimum of three-and-a-half feet high and made of brush, so fairly flexible if horse and rider clattered into one. In 'chase' races they could be anything from four-and-a-half feet and often solid. If a horse didn't have good technique it could end painfully for him and the rider. Like most horses, we were starting out down the path of hurdles. 'Let's see how we go with those before we step up,' Philip said. 'It's all about finding our feet.'

The law of diminishing returns predicted we'd have fewer syndicate members than previous outings. Bearing in mind some of them had little interest in horse racing, it was to be expected. The hardcore still travelled, though. There was a good day to be had regardless of the result.

As owners you got free tickets – but that was based on one or two owners per entrant. Most courses then allowed a dozen or so extra owners at half price or there-abouts. Any more needed to pay full price. For the first race nobody cared about the money. Euphoria was in the air; we all just wanted to see our boy. By race three there was more interest in penny counting. Poor Howard had to sort it. What he did was introduce a rolling system so everybody in turn would eventually receive a free ticket and a few at half price. If you didn't get in for gratis at one race then you would move up the waiting list for the next, and so on. That is if you still wanted to come. I have to say, three races in and we'd lost a third at least of the syndicate. *Another couple of races*, I thought, *and it'll just be me and Brian.* Still, as long as they paid their fees it was up to them how they supported the project.

Howard, though. Howard was irreplaceable. Indefatigable. It didn't matter whether the race fell on a weekday or a weekend, he always found the time to go along.

It was another strong field with eighteen riders. For once Mr McCoy didn't feature so Howard could relax – that is until he saw we were competing against a horse from the stable of Nicky Henderson, one of the most successful trainers in the sport. Keswick, ridden by Mick

Fitzgerald, was the standout for him despite the bookies having it at 40/1.

'I don't know what you're fussing about,' I said. 'Dream is 14/1 so he's obviously better. Have some faith now.'

The favourite on the day was Oscar Park from the stable of Colin Tinkler, ridden by Tom Doyle. Considering Dream had been the bookies' bet last time out I wasn't placing too much store on the numbers. Brian was, mind. In the days leading up to this race he ferreted around the internet trying to find the best odds on our boy. As he said, 'This £40 won't spend itself.'

Come the day, Dream Alliance was given the number four. In greyhounds, Brian told me, it mattered where you started. Trap one was better than trap six for example. On a racecourse the numbers were mostly for the officials really. At the start, the horses just milled around, you'd have to say. It was up to the jockey to get them pointing in the right direction at the appropriate time. If you wanted the inside line it was there for the taking. Similarly, if you wanted the outside you could have that too. Everything was fluid, which just added to the excitement.

According to the race programme, the going – that is to say, the turf conditions – were good to soft. 'Just right,' according to Philip. 'The harder the earth the more tiring he finds it.'

We all got ready. Brian had a few bets on the other races; even I put a fiver on something I liked the name of.

The beers were flowing again. The mood was good. And why not? Our horse had run just twice and come fourth and second. Going over the jumps, though, this was going to be make or break time.

The race got going and, of course, I got turning. There wasn't even a part of me that wanted to watch. I was a bag of nerves watching my boy just run in a straight line. The most dangerous thing he had had to do there was put one leg in front of the other. Today he was going to be jumping. We've all seen terrible things at the Grand National. Horses crashing through fences, horses landing on their necks, horses getting stuck in the hurdles. Some of them get away with it. Others get the screens put round them and a one-way visit from the vet. I had all the faith in the world in Dream but accidents happen. He only had to mistime one leap and the vet could be asking to put him down.

The early leaders, according to the track commentator, were Sunley Shines and Sativa Bay. I wasn't really interested. I was just thinking about that first hurdle.

What if he doesn't make it?

I don't think I took a breath for a good minute. The commentator flew through the list as they landed. They were all over, safe. Dream was in the middle. In a field of eighteen it wasn't terrible – and it wasn't great. But at least he was upright. As the next hurdles approached I held my breath again.

It didn't matter how many times he successfully nego-

tiated a hurdle, I had this horrible fear the next one could
be the match of him. Three from the end I should have
been confident. He was up into fifth from Mr Pointment,
Wee Robbie, Oscar Park and Sunley Shines. Another
hurdle and he took fourth. When they landed after the
tenth and final hurdle he was in third behind the favourite, Oscar Park, and Wee Robbie. Without looking I
knew he was giving it his all in the final straight. I could
picture him moving through the gears as he sniffed the
finishing line. It didn't sound like he was going to catch
the front two but no one was going to take his place
either. He powered home a fantastic third.

'Incredible,' Philip said. 'He never tired, he stayed the
course while those around him couldn't.'

There was a bit of cash for the bronze medal – £835.63
to be precise. Divided by twenty-three syndicate members that was about thirty-six quid each, so no quitting
the day job just yet. To be honest, we earned more from
our regular bet of £40 each way. A few of the more
well-off lads earned considerably more, let me tell you.
Several more noughts were involved, shall we say.

Footballers don't compete in the World Cup for the
cash. The same with our horse. My ambition had been to
create a true racer, raise him on my allotment and let him
take on the world. With our last bumper race out the way
I felt confident we were on course. To be honest, if
Dream hung up his shoes there and then, I'd have
achieved my goals.

But I looked into that boy's eyes down in the winners' enclosure and I knew he had more to give.

'You've got a win in you, I know it.'

It was just a question of when.

11

I Think Our Boy Has Fans

Saturday 28 January 2006. What a day for sport. Tennis great Amélie Mauresmo won the Australian Open, Bolton Wanderers put out FA Cup holders Arsenal in a 1–0 fourth-round win at the Reebok Stadium and tournament hosts Egypt put three past the Ivory Coast in the African Cup of Nations. Apparently, anyway. It all went over my head. I wasn't interested in events in Melbourne, Bolton or Cairo. I only had eyes for a little town about thirty-five minutes away to the east.

Chepstow, how do I love thee. It's in Wales for a start, so that makes it better than any other racecourse I'd been to. It also has some impressive history. During the war it was converted into an emergency airport for bombers. You have to admire that. Afterwards it was given the honour of hosting the Welsh Grand National after Caerleon racecourse shut down. Where it used to be one of the great flat races, over the years it's become a National Hunt staple. And that's what we were there for.

It was a Saturday so there were a few more bodies than we got at the midweek events. Not quite the cavalcade of minibuses leaving Cefn Fforest that we had for the first race but a presentable amount. Tony Kerby had his sandwiches again. Howard was there. Brian and I were there and so was our £40 bet.

Two miles, three furlongs, 100 yards and eleven hurdles. That was the day's challenge. The going was soft. According to Philip, anything that took it away from being a flat out sprint was a good sign. Our boy was a scrapper, not a rocket. More Colin Jackson than Linford Christie.

Once again, the man in the saddle for us was Richard Johnson. He hadn't let us down so far. We were right to trust Philip's judgement on that, like we trusted him on everything else. Not that he was the original choice, mind. With Richard initially scheduled to ride elsewhere Paddy Brennan was listed to be on board. When Richard's date was cancelled Philip moved him over.

The race was at 1.15. Its title was the Letheby & Christopher Maiden Hurdle. First prize was £3,415.64, obviously out of our range, but I did let myself have a glimpse at the rewards below. Second would earn £1.002.75, third £501.38 and fourth £250.43. But it was the places I craved. We'd had a fourth, a third and a second. If we could keep up that record I'd be chuffed to bits.

Because of the way the horse registration system worked, Dream was marked down as a five-year-old even

though it was a good four months till his real birthday. I
didn't know where that would leave him till I saw the
race card. There were five other horses the same age –
Principe Azzurro, Justice Jones, Sovietta, Red Echo and
Dayoff. The rest of the field ranged from six to eleven. I
asked Philip what it all meant.

'The youngsters will have the raw power but the older
horses will have the race craft. It's up to each jockey to
exploit his ride's potential as best he can,' he said.

Someone somewhere obviously expected something
similar to the last race at Newbury. For the second time
in four races, Dream Alliance was billed as the race
favourite. You'd need to put eleven pounds on him to win
ten. They could make him 1/1000 and it wouldn't stop us.
Our usual £40 was going on regardless.

The betting was just a happy distraction. Once the race
got going the money was the last thing on my mind. Back
Among Friends from Jim Old's stable ridden by Jason
Maguire was the early leader. Carew Lad at 100/1 was in
close contention. Exceptionnel and Montrolin were very
prominent in the commentary as well. Paul Nicholls'
Lunch Was My Idea had a big go around the seventh
hurdle but four out from the end, everything changed.
Dream took the lead and held it. Three hurdles to go
and I was crossing everything I had. He was no sprinter.
Anyone with a late spurt could put him under pressure.
But that didn't happen. Two hurdles to go, there was
fresh air between him and second place Principe Azzurro.

On a flat race you could relax at that point. Over the jumps it's a different proposition. It's so easy for horses to hurt themselves. On the second hurdle Justice Jones had blundered and unseated her rider. Sovietta and Blind Smart had both pulled up unexpectedly. Even the Jonjo O'Neill trained Tempsford, with A. P. McCoy on board, made a miscalculation. It made it over the hurdle all right but came down facing left – and that's where it ran. In National Hunt there are no easy moments. Until that horse crosses the line you could finish anywhere.

The commentator didn't seem to think so, though. He was screaming, 'It's Dream Alliance from Principe Azzurro, it's Dream Alliance, it's Dream Alliance.'

My God, he'd get anyone's heart racing.

I was beside myself.

'It's Dream Alliance by two lengths, Dream Alliance is going to do it, it's Dream Alliance, it's Dream Alliance . . . and . . .'

Come on, man, get it over with.

'Dream Alliance takes the win. Second is Principe Azzurro, third Carew Lad. It's the first win for the Alliance Syndicate's horse trained by Philip Hobbs.'

The whole thing was over in five and a half minutes. If you were watching it I imagine it flew by. Listening, it felt like an hour. By the end I felt I'd aged a year. Lord knows how the horse felt but I was drained top to bottom.

Every time we'd been out to watch or, in my case, *listen* to Dream's races, it had felt like a party. We were celebrating the fact we'd all got that far, me as a breeder, us as investors, everyone as working-class nobodies from the run-down coal towns of Caerphilly. We'd all been blown away by fourth. Third and second were the icing on the cake. So where did that leave coming first? I honestly didn't know what to think. Or do for that matter.

I lost track of the number of strangers I hugged. I wanted to dance with the world I was that happy. Brian and Howard were beside themselves as well. It's hard to explain the feeling. You want it, no question, and you do your damndest to get it, but when it comes along it's such a surprise. And a treat. And a shock. However you think you might react it goes out the window. Adrenaline takes over.

I'd barely had a glass of wine (it was only lunchtime, you know) but as we made our way down to the winners' enclosure I felt like I'd been on the booze all day. My mind was everywhere but where I needed it. I was staggering like an alky, giggly like a schoolgirl.

'Brian,' I said, 'I don't remember the whippets giving us this much pleasure.'

'No,' he said, 'nor the pigeons.'

'True. They were easier, mind.'

'Aye,' he laughed. 'That they were. And you could bear watching them and all.'

'I'm not sure I did,' I said. 'I only ever saw them land!'

The winners' enclosure had never seen anything like it. Fifteen of us bouncing around like kangaroos on candy bars. We didn't know what to do with ourselves. When the prize presentation commenced only Philip, ever the gentleman, retained any decorum. He took the trainers' prize and then it was time for the owner to go up. Or, in our case, the owners. I wondered whether we should draw straws to see who would collect the trophy and the cheque, but then I thought, *Sod it. We'll all go. We all deserve it. We're here, aren't we?*

In the photos that were taken you can barely see the trophy. Even Dream looks a bit dwarfed by the throng of well-wishers. There was talk about me going up to collect the trophy but how could I? Everyone owned an identical share. Nobody deserved the trappings of success over anyone else. The only thing that mattered was that the winners' cheque needed to end up with Howard. He was the one balancing the books until Kevin French got hold of them.

After fourth prize was handed out I assumed it was over. Then the master of ceremonies said, 'The winner of the breeders' prize is . . .'

When they announced the prize and read out 'The Rewbell Syndicate' as the winner, everyone looked at me.

'Go on,' Howard said, 'this one's for you.'

I was so chuffed. Going up there was like getting a big pat on the back. The cheque for five hundred quid was nice but nowhere near as valuable as that moment of recognition I got from my peers.

Yeah, I thought, *I bloody deserve this. That horse over there, the beauty that he is, he wouldn't be here today without me.*

It was true. Without the syndicate Dream would never have raced. But he'd still have been born and raised by me. He'd still have lived on the allotment, the difference being he'd have been there a lot longer.

On the way home it was one of those family 'roof down' moments. Brian was over the moon because of Dream winning and our little wager coming off. Me? I couldn't stop saying over and over: 'Janet Vokes: champion breeder.'

It was like I'd died and gone to heaven.

Winners, losers, you name it, Philip Hobbs had seen it all before. That didn't stop him being incredibly happy for us. He could see what it meant. We didn't have a stable of runners. We had one horse. All our dreams, all our hopes, rested on his mighty shoulders. After the race I said to Philip, 'What next?'

'Onwards and upwards, Janet. Next stop, Haydock Park.'

'Will he win that?'

'From what I've seen he'll have as good a chance as anyone else.'

I thought the same thing but hearing the expert say it meant more. To be honest, he could be a carthorse and I'd still think he was Red Rum. That's mother's love for you.

Haydock Park is another classic venue, again not too far from us. It's in Merseyside so at least the climate isn't too unfamiliar. It's a largely left-handed oval of a track, catering for National Hunt and flat runners. On 23 February 2006, they had the jumps out and our boy was down to leap over them.

February up Liverpool way isn't exactly the South of France. Our famous Welsh rain followed us all the way – via the cemetery as usual – up the M5, effortlessly merging with the Merseyside rain so common at that time of year. With a few races behind us now I was beginning to get the measure of the courses, in particular how they might affect our boy. When we listened to the radio on the way up and it said the going at Haydock was 'heavy' I knew exactly what it meant. I also knew what it might mean for Dream Alliance.

'Perfect,' I said to Brian. 'He's gonna lap this up.'

'Heavy' translates as 'boggy' or 'muddy'. It's as close as you can get to a swimming pool without the event being called off. Some horses thrive on the hard ground, they feel comfortable having solid earth beneath their hooves. Those are the ones most likely to go fastest on the flat. Other horses have different skills. They use their strength to cope with the elements, to get themselves over obstacles. Dream, I knew full well by then, was one of those. Give him a snorkel and flippers and he'd be happy.

What's good for the goose, mind, isn't always so perfect for the gander. Tsunami conditions might have suited Dream down to the soggy ground but over by the rails we were getting drenched. There was some cover under the main stands but Brian and I couldn't see the point in using it. We were owners so we should stay in the owners' enclosure. It seemed the right thing to do. The other few syndicate members had already made a beeline there.

There was another little advantage to the weather as well. For me, anyway. With the rain streaming down his face Brian found it difficult to follow the action over the way whereas I had as clear a race as usual listening to the track commentary.

Following his previous success, Dream was once again anointed with the tag of 'favourite'. According to the bookies he was 1/3 to come home first. In those conditions it seemed more of a lottery than usual; you'd need waterskis to guarantee anything. But, as Philip pointed out, you'll never meet a poor bookmaker. They know their markets top to bottom.

'Dream's only at the start of his career but, trust me, the money men have been watching him since day one. They don't like to be caught out. There isn't a horse running in the country at any level that they haven't been monitoring,' Philip explained.

'Blimey,' I said, 'so if they say he's favourite . . . ?'

'Then he is. Which means they're worried he could cost them money. And that's good.'

A quick scan down the race card showed a few familiar names. Noticeably Jonjo O'Neill's Tempsford was back, again ridden by A. P. McCoy. Personally, I hadn't seen anything from that combination to give me sleepless nights but Howard and Philip and seasoned gamblers like Tony Kerby continued to fear them.

'It's only a matter of time,' Howard said.

It wasn't a huge field. Only eight runners over ten hurdles around a distance of two miles, two furlongs and 191 yards. While it's easier to win from a smaller pool, coming fifth means you're only three from the back so it's not the shortcut you'd think. Richard Johnson was again in the hotseat. Before they got away he explained his race plan to us.

'I'll keep him in the pack until two thirds of the way then when we see the opening we'll step it up.'

'Just like you did at Chepstow?' I said.

'*Exactly* like we did at Chepstow. He's happier coming through.'

Some horses just have that knack of leading from the front. Others, like Dream, need something to chase, like a greyhound after the hare. They thrive on competition and they only really get that if they're staring at some-one's backside for half a race.

On paper all the horses were aged between four and seven. In truth, at five years old Dream was one of the youngest. Whether that would prove an advantage or a handicap we'd have to wait and see.

Finally, at 3.55, the Red Square Vodka 'Fixed Brush' Novices' Hurdle got going and the Merseyside punters got cheering. From a gambling point of view, the fewer the runners the more condensed the bets. Instead of spec-tators cheering on one of twenty-three horses, they were willing one of eight to get its arse in gear – which meant more cheers per runner. It's basic maths.

I don't normally pay much heed to what goes on around me when Dream is working. But, for the first time, I became aware of the 'whoops' every time his name came over the tannoy.

That's interesting, I thought, looking at Brian and the others who'd travelled up from home. *We're not the only ones betting on him. He's actually got some fans here.*

When you think of it, that's a bit weird. I never had anyone take an interest in Charlie or Lady or my other award-winning whippets. No one other than me and Brian ever put a penny on Will's Dream to win a pigeon race. It was a bit of a culture shock, if I'm honest, to sud-denly realize that other people were getting involved in what was basically my private hobby. I wasn't sure how I felt about that. Not for the first time I found myself thinking, *He's my horse, not yours.* With that thought in mind, I span around as the race began.

From the off, Casalani, ridden by Josh Byrne, made the running. Dream was there or thereabouts, as were Dino's Dandy, William Butler and Woodview. As the number of hurdles fell, the strengths of each horse came into play. My suspicions about the heavy soil suiting Dream appeared to be accurate. That boy liked a fight. Of that I was certain. The more unpleasant the environment, the more heart he put into tackling it. And with the rain bombarding everyone there was no danger of overheating.

Two hurdles from the end and Richard Johnson stepped it up as he'd done so many times before. Coming over the eighth of ten hurdles, according to my friend the commentator, Dream landed in first place and then held on to it over the final jumps like a dog with a bone. Casalani fell back behind Woodview who gave chase but when the finishing line was crossed after five minutes and seventeen seconds, it wasn't exactly a photo finish. Twelve lengths Dream was clear by. That is what you call a win.

There were so many reasons to celebrate. On a technical level Dream had been carrying more weight than anyone else. His 11s 9lbs made a mockery of third place Casalani's 10s 10lbs. That just showed how much extra he had in the tank.

In the winners' enclosure, though, it wasn't just pride I felt. As we collected our trophy and cheque for £4,554.20, the applause from the grandstands was overwhelming.

Shouting and hollering, whooping and clapping. When I looked up I saw so many smiling faces it was unreal. I'm not daft. They weren't congratulating us. It was all about Dream. It was an honour to know him.

'Howard,' I said, 'I think our boy has fans.'

'By the sound of it he's made a few of them a shilling or two,' he laughed.

That explained it, I suppose. Maybe a few had bet on him because they liked the name, the same way I gamble, but the rest I think were swayed by the odds. And the odds, according to the experts, had pitched Dream Alliance as favourite.

Which was exactly as I'd always seen him.

There was another prize for the winning breeder and for the second time in four weeks I picked it up. When I set off on the journey to breed a racehorse, this was all I was looking for. For all eternity, for as long as there are records, you'll be able to look up the race and see that the winning breeder was the Rewbell Syndicate, care of Janet Vokes. It was my name on there – not my father's, not my brother's, not my husband's. Kelly's daughter didn't breed this winner, nor Trevor's sister or Daisy's wife. I did. Janet Vokes. Me. My own person.

Five races into his career I couldn't see how Dream could do much better. Everyone I spoke to at the races held the same opinion. We'd all got on board for different reasons. Mine were particularly personal. Other people wanted a distraction from their lives. Some wanted to reclaim a missing spark from theirs. A few just wanted an excuse to have a jar or two and put a bet on every now and then.

The majority of the syndicate now chose to watch Dream's outings on TV or caught up with the result on the internet or in the newspapers later. That didn't make them any less valuable than Brian, Howard, even Gwyn, but it did suggest they weren't all in it for enjoyment alone. It was only after Haydock that it came to a head.

It was Howard who mentioned it first. He said he'd heard whispers – which I took to mean people had spoken to him directly – that there was some confusion over why we all shared the prize money from Dream but only I got the breeders' cheque. He knew the answer, mind. I was the breeder – it was my name on the registration. I'd done the work, bought the mare, researched the stallion. I put the building blocks in place for everything. More importantly, according to racing law, you can sell a horse but you can't sell your position as breeder. It's non-transferable. Every horse has a passport and Dream's lists me as breeder. Howard knew this, he was totally on the same page, and he made sure every person who questioned it got that answer. People are people though. You think you know them and then money gets involved and friendships take a back seat.

12

You've Got This

Despite being owners we also had the thrill of being out-siders. Philip's team ran the show, top to bottom. The syndicate was just along for the ride. Howard would get a call from the stables to say Dream would be running here or there and he'd spread the word and arrange the tickets. Shortly after Haydock, Howard called and said, 'Philip's been on. He's taking Dream to the Cheltenham Festival. It's a massive honour to get on the card there. The whole world will be watching.'

'Really?' I said. 'Well we better make sure we put a show on for them then.'

For many people, the Cheltenham Festival, with its twenty-four races over four days run on two separate courses, is the highlight of the National Hunt season. Its top prize, the famous Gold Cup, is second only to the Grand National in status and prize money. We weren't in that league but it felt like we were on the right trajectory.

Every race we took part in had a 'class' number. The best horses ran in Class 1 races. So far ours had mostly been Class 3. It was academic really. As long as we were racing like for like it didn't matter to me which band we were in. I just wanted a fair fight, that was all. But come March 2006, there was a definite bump up in expectations as Philip managed not only to get Dream into the Cheltenham Festival but on a Class 1 ticket.

And it was the race directly before the Gold Cup. Everyone who is anyone would be there to watch it.

Obviously I had the utmost faith in our trainer. He wouldn't put Dream anywhere the boy would struggle. That said, it was obviously going to be a harder field to negotiate. The fact the going was 'good' didn't necessarily help us. The more orthodox runners would enjoy the benefits of that more than Dream.

To the majority of the syndicate I don't think that much registered. Because it was the legendary festival and because our race was one of the support acts to the big climax, there was a noticeable upturn in attendance. Howard was on ticket duties as usual and divvied out the freebies to those who hadn't had one yet. As regulars, Brian and I had paid full price more often than not, and we'd done it without grudge. If your child is performing you'd pay to see him.

We were down for the 2.35 Spa Novices Hurdle. Our odds from the bookies said it all. 16/1 they reckoned. It didn't matter a jot that Dream had won his previous two outings, this was the big league and wow, didn't the prize money reflect that. First past the post would pick up a staggering £42,765! We'd have to win at Haydock ten times to get that much. Second place still got you sixteen-odd grand, then there were rewards of eight, four, two and one all the way down to sixth.

Brian, as usual, took the cautious route of betting each way. I think it was the sensible thing. There were plenty of horses here who knew what they were doing. And as for the jockeys, there were many recognizable names (if you subscribed to the Racing Channel, anyway).

'Black Jack Ketchum is the favourite,' said Howard. 'I'm not betting against our horse but that's the one to watch, I tell you now.'

The horses were in the parade ring and, my God, Black Jack Ketchum looked the part. I was thinking, *If he hasn't been gelded then I want my next horse to come from him.* That's how special he looked.

Looking with the eyes of a breeder, the parade ring for Dream's race was a bit daunting to say the least. It wasn't only Black Jack Ketchum, whose rider was A. P. McCoy, who stood out. Oscar Park was with us again, and he was looking strong, while Travino and Powerstation more than lived up to their short odds in the flesh. The only competitor that had run Black Jack Ketchum close recently was Powerstation. Luckily for us he was in our race as well.

'Maybe they'll wear each other out,' Brian said. 'Dream could creep up from behind.'

Everyone nodded sagely. But then I overheard a noisy group of spectators discussing their bets. They took things a stage further. One of them pointed at Powerstation. 'All we want is for that one to break his leg.'

I couldn't believe what I was hearing. How could someone say that about these beautiful animals? Of course I wanted Dream to win, without question. But not at any cost. The reason we, the syndicate, got up and running was because people liked the horses. You didn't go around wishing ill on the competitors. Maybe you'd hope for a stumble or a mistimed jump or the rider having a bad day. Something the horse would recover from. But an injury?

I really didn't like how heated other punters could be and that wasn't the last time I heard such sentiments exchanged. I sometimes wondered if people like that would be better off watching from the bookies.

Hand on heart, if they suddenly announced every race was going to be held at Cheltenham I might have just watched at home. It may be a festival known and respected all over the world but I hated it. You couldn't move for people. There were that many, if the crowd went right you couldn't go left. And if you did make it through you'd be queueing when you got there. Getting into the car park was horrendous, then into the ground itself took an age. The queue for the loos, my God they were a mile long, and as for the restaurants, don't even think about going in. They were booked solid and had been for months. Some people, Howard said, were already booking their lunch place for the following year. Unbelievable.

'How do they know they'll be coming?' I said.

'Oh, they'll be coming all right. Some people would miss their own funerals for Cheltenham.'

Even in our rarefied section of the ground where you could normally relax it was rammed. It was as though every horse was owned by a syndicate of one hundred and they'd all shown up. I think actually a fair few were on a bit of a jolly. The champagne was flowing. It reminded me of the party spirit we had going for Dream's first race. I was a bit sad that we seemed to have lost some of that over the course of eighteen short months.

I have to say the atmosphere in general was incredible. The noise of people chatting in the grandstands was deafening enough and that was before a horse had run. When the first race started it was like a bomb had gone off.

Howard turned to me and said, 'That was nothing. You come here for the first race of the festival and your ears will be ringing for weeks. They don't call it the "Cheltenham Roar" for nothing.'

Tony's comment about Black Jack Ketchum had been ill-judged but he was speaking from a gambler's point of view. When I watched the horses being led around the parade ring I did so as a proud owner but also as a breeder. I admired my boy, of course I did – he looked beautiful as ever – but so did plenty of the others. You can't go to the races and just think you have the best one there because there is no such thing as perfection. I would look at the other horses the way I looked at my pigeons and the dogs. I would ask myself, 'What do I need to improve next time? What's that horse got that our one hasn't?'

Even though you want your own to win you've got to see the faults in them to move forwards. That means seeing what's good in the others. It's never an either/or situation. There's no shame in being beaten by something better. The only real sin is not learning. In that respect the whole day was an education. Seeing so many top-class animals up close was like a masterclass in breeding. I'm no gambler but I could spot the ones I thought looked most promising before each race and, if I say so myself, they were usually in the mix at the end.

I'd like to say I enjoyed the race. I didn't really. I could barely hear the tannoy over the extremely passionate and, to be fair, knowledgeable crowd. And as for walking up and down like I normally did to work off nerves – I couldn't budge, could I? We were packed in that tight I couldn't see my feet, let alone move them.

A shade over five and a half minutes later, twelve hurdles on the 'New Course' having been negotiated, you'd have to say the best horse won. Black Jack Ketchum was impressive, they said. He'd tracked the leaders nice and smoothly then put the hammer down two fences out. No one could keep up. Travino was a distant third and even Powerstation in second looked like he was in a different race. Maybe that A. P. McCoy did know what he was doing. Dream meanwhile came home in sixth. One or two of the syndicate voiced their disappointment. Philip was more charitable.

'There were one or two mistakes out there today,' he said, 'but Dream gave it everything on quite hard ground and sixth is a very respectable result in a field of this quality.'

The organizers must have thought so too otherwise why pay out on that position? We got a very welcome cheque for £1,005 and that's not all – Brian was delighted to learn that because of the amount of runners our each-way bet went as low as Dream's position as well, so win-win.

We didn't have much choice but to watch the Gold Cup. We couldn't have moved if we'd wanted to. War Of Attrition took the tape and my word he looked the part. Even as we made our way back to the car, very slowly, I was thinking, *He's a lovely horse and a brilliant runner but I don't think we're that far off ourselves.*

Sometimes you can have too much of a good thing. If I could have arrived ten minutes before the race and left ten minutes after it ended I would have enjoyed it a hundred times more. It was fantastic to be there, and to have your horse running at the Cheltenham Festival is an honour, really, but I think it was almost too much of a day. Maybe I'd have felt differently with a win. Who can say? What I did know was that appearing at prestigious races wouldn't keep me happy for long.

I wanted more. And I knew Dream could give it to me. Unfortunately he had other ideas.

Our next day out was the Charity Day Novices Hurdle at Bangor-on-Dee, about twenty-five miles outside Chester, on 22 April 2006. Talk about a contrast to Cheltenham. There was me and Brian and that was about it. When the race got going I could have walked for miles away from the track, there was that much room. But Philip felt the course and the competition were just what we needed.

We had high hopes for the day. Tom O'Brien, another of Philip's jockeys, was making his debut on Dream. Brian and I both liked the cut of his jib.

'That boy will see us right,' Brian said.

Two hurdles into the race and it sounded like he was spot on. Dream was third, then second and, judging by the noise coming from Brian, about to make a serious push for first place.

'What's going on?' I shouted to Brian behind me. I wanted to know.

'He's doing it, that's what. He's in the lead!'

For four more hurdles Dream led. When he landed after the eighth, with four to go, he was pulling away from the other riders. Again I was in Brian's ear.

'What's he doing now?'

Without taking his eyes from the track for a second, he said, 'He's about three lengths clear, I'd say.'

'Come on, boy,' I whispered, 'you've got this.'

And then suddenly it was all over.

Brian swore, he screamed and of course I had to turn round then. He was staring over at the course but he wasn't watching the runners.

'What's going on?' I shouted.

Without saying anything he pointed to the eighth hurdle.

'Dream's down,' he said.

I'd never felt so sick.

'What happened?'

'I don't know. He cleared the fence.'

'Is he going to be all right?'

'Wait!' Brian exclaimed. 'It looks like he's still going. But there's no Tom.'

My stomach was in my boots. When I spotted him galloping towards the finish line I began to cry. It was like watching those baby steps he'd taken the day we first laid eyes on him. He was unsure but he was strong. It was just a shame Tom wasn't still on board. I had really been dreading the sight of the vet arriving. That sounds wrong, I know. I was quite the racing novice before we started down the road with Dream Alliance but there was one thing I did know about the sport: if a horse gets injured during a race and can't use its leg, it gets put down. Often there and then on the racecourse. They get the course vet over, they get the tent up around it and it's over in seconds. You go from being a racehorse owner to having a dead pet on your hands.

'I hope he's alright,' I was saying, 'please let him be okay.'

Catching up with Tom after the race it was exactly as Brian called it: Dream hit a pothole and that was that. He'd gotten straight back up and there was no lasting damage. What a relief.

'A terrible shame,' Tom said, 'because we had a win on our hands there.'

That's jockeys for you, always thinking about the work. I was just grateful Dream was okay. Of course, if he did have a permanent injury it would speed up him coming back home to live with me. Every cloud has a silver lining.

Bangor was pretty much the end of the racing season anyway, so we had a few months to get Dream ready again for autumn and the next chapter, which suited me and Brian just fine. We needed all the time we could get right then because we had an allotment to get ready.

Our new horse was coming home.

13

A Long Way from Home

By the time he ran at Cheltenham Festival in 2006, Dream Alliance was five years old. During that time his mother Rewbell hadn't exactly been twiddling her thumbs. Chris Nebercheck, who had looked after Dream before he'd moved to Philip's, was so taken with him – or 'Ben' as he called him during their time together – that he asked if there were any more like him back on our allotment.

'No,' I said, 'but that could change if you want.'

'If you produce another one I'd certainly buy it.'

In 2003 I introduced Rewbell to M'Bebe and once again the mare didn't let us down. Bouncing Bean, a beautiful filly, was born in 2003 just as her big brother was making his debut at Newbury. I have to admit, I enjoyed the whole process of breeding Bean, but it was very time-consuming. After she was born, I wasn't sure whether I would do it again.

But in 2004, with Dream out injured after racing at Newbury, it gave me some time to myself. *Why not?* I thought. *Otherwise I'll just be going from Kelly's daughter to Dream's breeder.*

As with Dream, it was another American horse on his travels that we used. Beat All, then at Mickly Stud in Shropshire, was just starting out on his new career but he'd produced some minor winners already. I had every hope we could produce a new colt who could join the club.

The foal that arrived in April 2006 ended up being a filly but we still had everything in place. The plan was simple: she'd live with us initially on the allotment then go off for training to a local yard run by John Flint at first and if she showed potential maybe over to Sandhill – and it would all be funded by a syndicate once again organized by Howard. I felt I knew what I was doing this time round and thankfully by then Dream Alliance had convinced enough other people the same. There were a few names in common but mainly the new syndicate was populated by different people, all drawn in by the success of the big brother. It seemed obvious to maintain the connection so even though she was Dai Bando at home, when it came to registering her for racing we went with Recurring Dream.

I just hoped she'd do better than her brother was managing at that moment.

I had thought a return to the scene of Dream's best result could be a good omen. Chepstow on 21 October 2006 might just have been the fillip he needed after struggling at the Cheltenham Festival and his fall at Bangor. It wasn't to be. According to the reports he got bogged in the pack, found some speed at the seventh hurdle but never kicked on. Even Richard Johnson couldn't get a burst out of him and he came in a sluggish and tired-looking fifth. I thought perhaps he could have been nervous of finding another pothole, but Johnson White said he'd been running with confidence at Sandhill. Howard reported back that Philip himself was also optimistic at the next syndicate meeting.

'Philip isn't worried – he said after Cheltenham and the fall Dream's feeling his way back. There are bound to be cobwebs. He still picked up £421 at Chepstow so it wasn't a disaster. Judge him on the next race at Exeter, he reckons.'

Like everything uttered by that man, it seemed eminently sensible to me.

Philip was so confident that Dream was coming back into form that the Exeter meeting he signed us up for on 17 November was a bit different. The clue was in the name: the Nash Dash Novices' Chase. Chases – or steeplechases – have very specific differences to hurdle races. The obstacles you have to negotiate can include water jumps and open ditches often tucked behind a giant fence. Not only are these fences taller than the hurdles Dream had been jumping in his races so far, but they're harder, sturdier and more likely to hurt on the way over if you don't get it right. If I'd ever fancied being a jockey – which I hadn't – this would have put me off, no question. And that's before you considered the seventeen-strong opposition.

'Are you sure he's ready to step up, Philip?' I asked.

'He'll need to if we want to take a serious stab at one of the Nationals or the bigger Cheltenham races.'

The Welsh Grand National, he said, fell in December. It was probably too early for him that year but it should be a definite target for 2007, Philip said.

The Welsh National. *What an achievement that would be.* Still, December 2007 was a long way off. *Let's not run away with ourselves . . .*

Captain Aubrey was quickest off. He led the early fences until Dream Falcon got his nose in front – or 'headed' as the experts call it. Kilcarty was right behind, dicing with our boy for fourth. By the sixth fence the commentator declared that fight over: 'Dream Alliance has taken the lead.' He'd been tracking the front-runners and finally got his sprint on. The question was, how long could he keep it up?

The next nine jumps were excruciating to listen to. Dream was holding on but only just. Tidy he wasn't. Three from the end I thought, *He's not used to leading this long. He's not going to make it.*

I was on Brian's shoulder, nagging him. Nothing different, the usual questions.

'What's he doing? How's he going?'

'Look for yourself, woman!'

'You know I can't! And definitely not this one. Those fences look evil. What if he has a fall?'

Somehow Brian managed to listen to me and follow the commentary without his eyes once leaving the track. I don't know how he did it.

Two fences out and I heard him relax.

'They're fading,' he said, not to anyone in particular.

'Who's fading?' I asked.

'Everyone but our boy. He's pulling away. Two fences to go. I think he's going to do it.'

And he was right. It was a struggle physically and the jumps themselves were a bit ragged, but by the time Dream crossed the line in six minutes and ten seconds, there were eight clear lengths between him and runner-up Dream Falcon.

First place on his debut chase. That was pretty special and I told him so as soon as I could. Being back in the winners' paddock felt good, I can't lie. The £7,807.20 prize was welcome; the breeder's prize meant more, if I'm honest, especially with Recurring Dream sitting at home. The award that meant most, though, was having a fit-again horse standing next to me after showing the world what he's made of.

I couldn't have been prouder.

The Welsh Grand National runs every year the day after Boxing Day, so come 27 December that's what my TV was tuned to. Dream wasn't down to run again that year but now Philip had planted the seed of such a big race I thought I'd check it out. Even if I was a year early. It was run at Chepstow, which I liked as a venue. More importantly, Dream liked it there as well. *Fingers crossed for 2007.*

Dream's racing year started at another track he had enjoyed – very recently. Come New Year's Day 2007 we were back at Exeter for the 2.25 Hatch Marquee Hire Novices' Chase. It was a slightly different circuit to before – about a quarter of a mile longer but with two of the seventeen fences omitted. Considering Dream won it at the last two fences in November I wasn't convinced the decision was in our favour.

For some reason the field was smaller than usual, just six horses lining up to claim the £7,807.20 top prize. That had to be good for us, I decided, and so it seemed. Blue Splash got away tidily but after two fences Dream was ahead. And there he stayed until the penultimate fence when Blue Splash suddenly came past. I don't know if Dream could have done any more – Brian said he made a small mistake at the thirteenth but then the winner had done the same the fence before. It's to be expected on such a heavy track. What I can say is I was as happy as always to give him a hug in the winners' enclosure. You could see he'd run his heart out.

'That's all anyone can ask,' I said.

And yet, when you know your horse has a heart as big

as his, watching Dream Alliance come anywhere other than the top rung should have set alarm bells ringing. Looking back, there was a distinct pattern. After back-to-back wins at Chepstow and Haydock, he'd found the going at the Cheltenham Festival too hard and, for two races after that, either side of the sport's summer break, he'd kind of disappeared. And now he was doing it again.

Two tough Exeter races had taken their toll. When he lined up at Huntingdon twenty-four days later it was to finish an unremarkable fourth. *Out of four.*

It could have been a different story. He led for most of the race but mistakes at the eighth and ninth fences allowed the others to swarm past. It was disappointing, but while they're giving prize money for fourth position I refuse to call it 'last'.

At Warwick on 20 March 2007 he went one better: third out of four. Again, if you're being positive you could say that's a 25 per cent improvement. Tom O'Brien was riding this time but he still couldn't get a tune.

Things were getting desperate now. I think even Philip was beginning to get nervous. With a return to Cheltenham around the corner we had one more race for Dream to try to run some form back into his legs.

It was my first time at Ascot. Usually you associate it with the big hats, Ladies' Day and flat racing, but it also hosts some important steeplechase fixtures. The Thames Hospicecare 2007 Appeal Novices' Handicap Chase may or may not be one of them – but it would have felt a damned sight more important if we'd won. Or at least placed in the top five. Coming in sixth from seven starters was thoroughly dispiriting but at least we earned £174 for the effort, which is £174 more than seventh placed Notanotherdonkey picked up. There's always someone worse off than you . . .

With April approaching it didn't look good for Cheltenham. Not one bit. I had to believe, though, that our luck would change soon. It had to. After his previous lean spell Dream had come back with a vengeance. I was desperate for him to do it again. To show everyone what he was capable of. We all were.

You can understand how people think sometimes they're cursed. Come the morning of 19 April we were on our way to Cheltenham and I was about to think it myself.

The more popular tracks always brought a few syndicate members out and this time we were travelling with Howard's brother Gwyn and a fella from the working men's club, Gerwyn Evans. His mother used to own the garage at the top of the village. I always got on with Gerwyn. That's why I used to turn a blind eye every time I heard he missed a payment. A number of people had the odd late payment here and there. Mistakes happen and money gets tight for different people at different times, so the understanding was that anybody who missed three months was out. A few times Gerwyn went over three months and I never said anything. But I would take him aside on the quiet when he came in the bar and say, 'You need to pay me today, young man, or you're out.' And usually he did.

We were in the car when I got a call from Philip. Trainers are always at the tracks early to get the horses ready. But on this particular day Philip hadn't liked what he'd seen.

'The ground is solid,' he explained, 'rock hard. I'm phoning to ask if you want me to pull him out?'

When I thought back to the disastrous trio of races we'd just endured, did we really need another black mark blotting the copybook?

'Trust me, Janet,' he said, 'there's no shame in withdrawing. A lot of other horses have already gone.'

I said, 'Philip, if it was your horse what would you do?'

'I'd withdraw to fight another day.'

'Look, it's not my decision,' I said. 'I'll call you back.'

I explained the situation to Brian, Gwyn and Gerwyn. As the only ones travelling it seemed fair they'd have a say. I quickly regretted it.

'Can't we just bring him out and canter around?' Gerwyn said. The idiot.

In a way, that crystallized my thinking. I called Howard and said, 'We're pulling out.'

'Not a problem,' he said. 'I'll make the arrangements. But what are we going to do instead? Is Dream's season ending on this terrible run?'

'Leave it with me, Howard. Philip will know.'

It turned out that Philip had been originally in two

minds about Cheltenham. There was another race up in Perth, Scotland, around the same time, which he actually thought might have been better. At the end of the day, though, with Dream not pulling up trees right then, Cheltenham was a much shorter journey.

'I'll see if I can get us back on at Perth,' he said.

When he rang back it was one of those good news/bad news conversations. The good news was that Dream was entered for Perth on 26 April. The bad news was that the deadline day for admissions to the original race had passed – so Philip had entered us into a more challenging, higher-standard event instead.

'I think he can do it,' Philip said. 'It might even be what he needs right now.'

'I'll take your word for it,' I said. 'At least we'll have a nice day or two away.'

Unsurprisingly no one else from the syndicate made the long journey from Wales. But one member was already there.

Gordon Hogg lives in Scotland so we met him at the racetrack. He was over the moon we'd made the journey. He was aware that Dream hadn't been his best recently but honestly I think he was that happy to see his horse on his home soil he wouldn't have minded him walking round.

We went to the stables at the track and introduced Gordon to Tom O'Brien and generally showed him what was what. He'd never seen Dream this close. I was so busy chatting I didn't take much notice of Brian. Suddenly he was animated.

'What's got up with you?' I asked.

'I need to phone Howard and the others.'

'Why, what's wrong?'

'Nothing's wrong. I want to tell them to put a bet on our boy. I'm telling you now, he's going to win today.'

There are a lot of things I'd doubt my husband's knowledge of but not this. He knows horses and he knew Dream. Two minutes alone with that horse and he could see there was only one result our boy was going to accept today, and that was to finish ahead of the rest.

Of course, nobody else believed him. More fool them, I say.

Our friends weren't the only doubters. On our way back to the spectators' area we stopped for a cup of tea. The fella serving picked up on the accents, obviously.

'You're a long way from home, Taff,' he said. 'What you up here for?'

I turned the accent up a notch for his benefit.

'We've got an 'orse, you see.'

'Oh, you have, have you. Is it going to win?'

'You better believe it. Put your takings on it, I would.'

He laughed. I had the same conversation half a dozen times with hot-dog vendors, bar tenders, programme sellers, same result each one.

'They think we're mad,' Gordon said. 'I don't blame them.'

'Wait till they hear about the horse coming from an allotment.'

We went back to the side of the track and Gordon said, 'Where are we going to stand?'

I could see what appeared to be a private enclosure at the edge of the owners' area, right by the trackside. 'Look,' I said, 'there's room for us in there – and it's by the finishing post. Let's try and get in.'

So that's what we did, creeping in like naughty school-kids doing a bunk. As long as we didn't draw attention to ourselves we shouldn't be discovered, I thought.

The race was the stanjamesuk.com Perth Festival Handicap Chase with the Kilmany Cup at stake. Show time was 4.15 and the weather was already turning by the time it came around. At least the ground was soft, though.

It had been such a lovely day already I wouldn't have minded too much if Dream wasn't feeling it for whatever reason. But I had every confidence he was going to deliver. That confidence was shattered a minute into the race. Not being surrounded by other screaming punters in our enclosure, there was no problem hearing the commentary. The problem was, I didn't like what I was hearing.

They'd been over three jumps and I hadn't heard Dream mentioned once. Four jumps and still nothing. It was terrible. I ran over to Brian.

'Has he fallen? Can you see him? The commentator hasn't mentioned him once.'

Brian had his field glasses so he got focusing on the other side of the course as best he could.

'He's definitely there,' he said, 'I can see Tom.'

Even as we were arguing the commentator said, 'And that's Mr Woodentop out in front, Mr Woodentop from the favourite Lothian Falcon, then it's . . .' and off he went through the top ten, never once mentioning Dream.

Oh, this is terrible, I thought. *Maybe he's been disqualified.*

Suddenly the tannoy announcer interrupted his own flow and said: 'Sorry, that's not Mr Woodentop in the lead – it's Dream Alliance.'

He'd been getting the name wrong the whole race!

Oh, you should have heard us scream. I was beside myself. Gordon was doing a jig and Brian was whooping like he was summoning rain. I felt like I'd been put through a tumble-dryer of emotions already and it wasn't getting any better. As the race reached its final stages I was thinking, *He's going to do this. He's going to do this.* I was pacing up and down as usual, but luckily we were by the winning post. As I heard the commentator getting more and more high pitched and excited I thought, *You know what, I'm going to watch the end of this.*

For the first time ever I was going to watch my horse. I just prayed I wasn't going to jinx anything by looking.

I turned around to face the track. I hung over the railing and I waited and I waited to cheer my darling horse home.

And he never came.

I looked at Brian, he looked at Gordon, we all looked at each other.

'Where's Dream?'

It wasn't just our horse that didn't come by. None of them materialized.

I turned to the fella nearest to me and said, 'Excuse me, I thought this was the winning line?'

'Oh aye,' he said, 'but not for this race. This is the hurdles finish. The chase one is over there.'

No wonder it's so bloody empty.

It didn't matter, mind, the result was still the same. Dream Alliance won the race and I could honestly still say I hadn't seen my horse race a single yard! The winning margin was twelve lengths, the winning time nearly six and a half minutes and the winning cheque £25,052!

'We're rich!' Brian yelled.

'I know,' I said, 'twenty-five grand isn't bad for an afternoon's work.'

'I'm not talking about the prize money,' he said. 'I'm talking about our winnings. £500 we got!'

We were running and jumping like teenagers and couldn't wait to get to the winner's enclosure. On the way I heard some shouting above the general noise. A couple of the hot-dog vendors and that were waving at us.

'You came through, you beauty!' the tea guy said.

'Did you put your takings on like I told you?'

'No, my wife would kill me if I had. But I won a few bob on your horse, don't you worry.'

It was like a carnival and when I finally got my hands on Dream I think the tears flowed as much as the champagne. Tom O'Brien looked exhausted but exhilarated at the same time. I don't think he'd ever really had a glimpse of what Dream could do. He was in no doubt now.

14

You're Spoiling It for the Rest of Us

Time and horses wait for no man and while we were still celebrating Dream's incredible race at Perth, Philip was plotting the next phase.

It was, he declared in his usual understated way, a decent way to end the season. 'A return to form, a return to winning – and in such a good quality race as well. In fact, I think,' he said, 'we should up the ante next time. We're running out of mountains to climb.'

After what we'd just witnessed – *nearly* – with our own eyes, I felt Dream could race against a Formula 1 car and still hold his own. We were buzzing that much.

'What have you got in mind, Philip?' I asked.

He paused. 'You know, I don't think it's out of the question to have a stab at the Hennessy.'

'That's amazing,' Brian said. Gordon was equally impressed.

Me? I couldn't wait for the next challenge.

*

Newbury Race Course hosts some wonderful and prestigious events. None of them come close to the Gold Cup. The 'Hennessy' is a long steeplechase race: three miles and two furlongs, with twenty-one fences ranging from two-bar obstacles to ditches hidden behind the fence. For your efforts there's £85,530 for the winner. Sadly the association with Hennessy Cognac ended recently after a record-breaking sixty years, having been passed down through eight generations of the famous family business. In 2017, a new sponsor came on board. But anyone who knows about horse racing, about the classics, knows it as the Hennessy.

I, for one, was looking forward to making its acquaintance.

Large rewards like this one attract the best and I'm not joking when I say we could smell the money when we arrived. We were rubbing shoulders with people who would be putting bets on worth more than I earn in a month, a year maybe. It didn't bother me, though. Dream would be getting our £40 each way as usual and we'd be happy to get anything back.

Ideally we'd have got an earlier race in beforehand to blow the cobwebs off after summer, but a foot problem discovered by the trainers at the start of the season meant a few weeks' R&R was the wiser option. So, come 1 December 2007, we were going in cold. The only good news was some of the race's big hitters were coming in fresh as well. The 9/2 favourite Snowy Morning, trained by Willy Mullins and ridden by A. P. McCoy, hadn't run since Punchestown the previous spring. The 5/1 Denman, from Paul Nicholls, hadn't run since earlier, at Cheltenham, while John Quinn's 8/1 Character Building hadn't been out since Ayr the same day we were in Perth. Of the most fancied pre-race bets, only Abragante at 6/1 and New Alco at 13/2 had run at all that season, at Wincanton and Carlisle respectively, where they each emerged winners.

Looking through the race card and the recent history of horses of that calibre I was happy that we were at 16/1. Tom O'Brien was on Always Waining at 20/1 but there were horses at 33, 40, 50, even 100/1. Our odds were low enough to be a little nod to where we'd come from, what we'd achieved, but high enough to keep our feet on the ground. There were some serious racers about to line up. Only a fool or a cockeyed optimist would expect anything more than a low placing at best.

'View it as another Cheltenham Festival,' Howard said. 'We're really going up a notch in class here today.'

I saw that soon enough with my own eyes. Flicking through the race card and the horses' histories only told part of the story. When they came out before the race into the parade ring you got the full picture.

I'd like to say I only had eyes for Dream Alliance but as gorgeous as he looked, he was surrounded by beauties. It was like a Miss World for horses in that paddock. A few of them made Black Jack Ketchum look a bit ordinary. I thought, *Well, Philip did say this was for the crème de la crème.*

One horse definitely caught my eye, the second favourite, Denman. I knew from the race card and from Brian that he was one strong horse and he looked it. Dark bay, tall as you like, and front leg muscles that rippled even as he stood still.

'He's front-powered when he runs,' Howard pointed out. 'You can tell.'

There's a downside to having a natural advantage, of course. The Hennessy Cognac Gold Cup Chase was listed as a 'handicap' – which meant the strongest runners got a bit more weight to carry than some of the others. Although I think even Philip raised an eyebrow when he saw Denman was carrying 11s 12lb. When you think Dream only had 10s 7lbs and Character Building got away with ten flat, you had to feel sorry for him. Or did you?

'He's obviously good enough to deserve it,' Brian said. 'We'll have to watch this one.'

'I won't be watching anything,' I said. 'I tried it at Perth and it didn't work. I'm taking that as an omen.'

'Well, as long as you're not bothering me,' he said, 'we'll have a good race.'

Richard Johnson had been due to ride for us but he'd broken his leg so Jamie Moore was in the hot seat. If he was nervous he didn't show it. We wished him luck, of course, then left him to race while we went off to go doolally in the owners' enclosure. That was the formula. It had got us that far and I didn't see why it wouldn't continue. In any case, it was the only plan we had.

About fifteen of the syndicate were at Newbury with us, many of them with their partners, so it was a decent turnout. It reminded me of the first time we'd visited the place. I couldn't remember a party atmosphere quite like that in the three years since. I realized I missed it. Things are always better in a crowd.

Of course, it depends on the *right* crowd. Every coin has two sides, and the downside of participating in upper echelon events was you got to mingle with owners and the like who considered themselves a bit upper echelon as well.

My kind of people are the ones serving the teas and the hot dogs at Perth. They're the lads and lasses in our working men's clubs. Salt of the earth they may be, but straight as a die. Though we never really experienced any snobbery, it was obvious we weren't like the usual owners!

It seemed to take forever for 2.40 to come round. Then finally the starter got it going and we were off.

'Good luck, my boy,' I said, and promptly went for my walk. Up and down, up and down I went, stopping, straining to hear the commentary. At some races you can hear the hooves when they come by on the first lap, but not here. For all their airs and graces and money, the Newbury clientele were no different from the rest of us when things got going, leaping like lunatics when their horses got off. A Gold Cup at stake affects everyone the same. Especially if you've got a wager on. Whether it's 10p or ten grand, you'll be bouncing if your horse gets a sniff at the prize. It just adds a bit of flavour to the race, having someone to cheer.

A quarter of the way round, the commentator was saying the same names. Sir Rembrandt, Snowy Morning, Denman, Character Building, D'Argent and Dream. That sounded about right to me. I'd be happy if they came home in that order.

Halfway round and our lot from the syndicate were making themselves heard above the rabble.

'Brian, what's going on? What's he doing?'

'Look for yourself, woman! He's moving up.'

I was tempted to peek but I couldn't. What if I jinxed it? What if he fell? By the time they reached the water jump the volume from the general crowd went up a notch. I didn't even think that was possible. One circuit to go and the obvious crowd favourite Denman was asserting himself. He took the lead, but Sir Rembrandt had the inside line on the left-hand bend. Dream was watching it all happen from a couple of lengths back.

Heading into the last lap there were three of them together. Denman, Sir Rembrandt then Dream. Denman, by the sound of it, was not going to be beaten. But Dream hadn't finished either. Sir Rembrandt had done its best but was tiring. Five fences to go and clear at the front was Denman – but in second place was Dream.

Our lot weren't to be outdone by the Denman masses. We went wild. So wild a man kitted out in tweed said to Brian, 'Would you mind calming down, old chum? You're spoiling it for the rest of us.'

Brian said, 'Calm down? My horse is the only one close enough to smell Denman's arse. You'd be bloody jumping up and down if he was yours. Maybe you should stick to watching on television next time.'

But had he spoken too soon? We'd fought off one challenge but suddenly the commentator was saying Dream was coming under pressure. Character Building was sniffing his shot at glory.

Coming into the second fence from last it was all to play for.

The crowd and owners were going crazy, willing their horses on. The roar that greeted Denman clearing the fence wouldn't have pleased Mr Tweed. Two seconds later he definitely wasn't happy. According to the cheers from Brian, Dream had obviously made it over too, but not as convincingly.

'He's tiring,' Brian said. 'That fence took a lot out of him.'

'He'll be all right,' I said, still not looking. 'He won't give up.'

And he didn't. Whatever the rest of the field threw at him, Dream responded. By the time he crossed the finishing line he was twelve lengths behind Denman – but the same distance clear of third.

You'd think we'd won the thing. The truth was, everyone at Newbury knew they'd witnessed – or in my case, heard – something very special in Denman. He'd performed as well as I knew he would the second I'd laid eyes on him in the parade ring. As my father said when I phoned seconds after the finish, 'It's no shame to come home behind that horse by twelve lengths or twenty.'

Eighteen horses of very good pedigree, one a legend in the making. And we'd come home second. £32,085 was the reward. Not a bad haul at all. And yes, at 16/1 Brian was more than delighted with the payout from the bookies.

The tweed brigade was still hanging around when we left so I said loudly, 'Come on, let's go congratulate our second-placed horse and then get back to our slag heaps.'

Sometimes after a race you get the feeling the horse could do it all again if you asked him. That wasn't the case at the Gold Cup. When I saw Dream in the winners' enclosure he looked spent. He'd given everything, just like I'd always asked of him. In hindsight, that should have been a warning. The clues were there, we just didn't know where to look.

The truth is, our tails were up and as far as the Alliance Syndicate was concerned, it was onwards and upwards. Plenty of them said very complimentary things to me, which was nice.

Gwyn made me laugh, saying, 'I thought the Gold Cup would be a booze-up with my mates and not much more. You ruined that for us.'

Flattering as it all was, a day or two later it was out of my head. I was more interested in the future than the past, and the future for Dream and all of us was something quite special.

'It's the Welsh National next,' Philip announced. 'And I think we've got a serious chance.'

'My God,' I said to Brian. 'The Welsh. This could really put us on the map.'

He nodded. 'Something tells me we're going to have a very, *very* good Christmas.'

15

They're Going to Shoot Him

We had a lovely Christmas with the family and Boxing Day was meant to be more of the same. The truth is, we were all only half present. The next day was the Welsh Grand National and that's all Brian and I could think about. The kids kept having to snap their fingers when we drifted off.

Finally 27 December 2007 arrived, and once again a convoy set off down the M4 to Chepstow. After what they'd witnessed at Newbury the syndicate had every expectation of more of the same, and I'm not just talking about our boy. Following Dream's results on the TV or in the newspapers will give you the facts but it won't tell you about the atmosphere, the wonder of seeing those great beasts racing, the unforgettable sound of the hooves pounding the earth, even the smells of the place. It all adds to the magic of the day and now they'd had a taste they wanted more.

No one wanted it more than me. We went through the

usual pre-race ritual of visiting Brian's parents' graves, going to see the horses, getting our bets on, getting a prime vantage point, and waited to see what Dream could do. He was listed as second favourite at 6/1 so obviously the bookies were hopeful. Only National Hunt legend Ruby Walsh on Gungadu was more popular, at 4/1. Sir Rembrandt was back as well, at 20/1.

At 2.05 the race got underway and I knew immediately from Brian that things weren't going to plan.

'What is it?' I said.

'Something's wrong. He's too far back.'

It didn't improve. As the race went on Dream held station towards the rear. By now I was relying on my husband for all my news because as a rule commentators don't bother with horses that far back. At the thirteenth Brian winced.

'He clipped it,' he reported, 'but he's okay.'

Not for long. At the fifteenth Richard Johnson made the decision to retire the horse. I couldn't blame him. Something was obviously up. Dream just didn't want to be there. Interestingly Sir Rembrandt pulled up as well.

Back at the stables Philip and his team had a good look under the bonnet but found nothing. He had tests done on Dream's legs, his back, all over. The vets found no sign of injury. We had to presume it was one of those things, they said.

'The best you can do is wait to see what happens next time he races.'

It was sound advice so we did wait, and we did see what happened the next time he raced – and no one could really believe it.

I doubt the bookies could either. We were at Exeter on 10 February 2008 and clearly they hadn't heard about Chepstow because Dream was established early on as 2/1 favourite. I admired the confidence they had in him although it did impact on Brian's winnings.

Early on, though, things were looking and sounding good. Dream tracked the early leaders and held steady before making his move. Once he got first place it was just a question of how much he would win by.

'And it's Dream Alliance leading by two lengths,' the commentator said. Then it was three lengths.

There were four clear lengths between Dream and the horse in second when the crowd let out a gasp. There were even a few screams from our lot. I span right round. It was instinctive.

'What's happened?' I said. 'Where is he?'

Brian was almost too shocked to speak.

'Well, Dream just crossed the finish line but Richard's on the floor over there.'

A second later my daughter called. She was watching on TV.

'What did he do that for?' she asked.

'Do what?' I said.

'It looked like he just jumped off.'

When I told Brian he said, 'What, he did a Frankie Dettori?'

All I knew about the Italian was his famous flying dismounts – but they were usually from a stationary horse. Richard had come off at 40mph.

'I can't see him, can you?' he said. 'He could have killed himself at that speed.'

'Is Richard all right?' I asked Sasha on the phone. 'Can you see him?'

'Yeah, he's walking. He'll live. It's Dream I'm worried about. They've got to catch him now!'

While Philip was trying to sort that out, I said to his wife, Sarah, 'Do you think this is related to Dream not running so well last time?'

'I doubt it,' she said. 'In my experience when a rider gets unseated it's normally his fault not the horse's. You'll have to ask Richard.'

'I can't tell you,' Richard said when we caught up with him later. 'We were leading and I felt him stumble and I thought, *He's going to roll*, so I had to get off before he took me with him.'

If it was that or being flattened by a 70-stone juggernaut travelling at 40mph he probably did the right thing.

'At least you're all right,' I said. 'Better luck next time, eh?'

*

It seems silly to talk about luck, but after a mysterious non-finish, then this weird accident while Dream was leading the race, I felt we deserved a change in fortunes. I hoped Kempton Park in a fortnight's time would be our day.

We arrived in buoyant spirits, let's say. It was rare for Philip to enter Dream in two races so close together, so he must have been optimistic. I certainly was. My boy had had Exeter in his pocket. No one could have beaten him if his pilot had stayed on board. From everything I'd seen on the gallops at the stables he was in magical form. I couldn't wait for 3.15 to come round. The *Racing Post* was the race sponsor. It's a great paper for the sport and I was looking forward to featuring heavily the next day.

Before the race we had a chat with Richard as normal in the parade ring. He explained his plan, which was essentially what it always was. Basically, Dream likes to be in the chasing pack, third or fourth ideally, before he makes a move over the last fence or three. Go too early and he'll tire. He's not one of those who enjoys leading from the front.

'I will keep him handy and see how the race pans out and towards the end if he's got it we will go,' Richard said.

'Sounds good to me, lad,' Brian said. We wished him well and off we went to the posh stands.

Well, 3.15 came, the starting rope went down and I couldn't believe what I heard.

'Dream Alliance is out of the blocks and he doesn't look like being caught.'

'Brian,' I said, 'what's going on?'

'I'll tell you what's going on: he's shot off like a bat out of hell.'

'He can't lead the whole race.'

'Tell Dream and Richard that.'

I really hoped that I would be surprised but obviously it was only a matter of time before the inevitable occurred. There were only eighteen fences but our race was over by the fourteenth. Dream was so far behind the last horse Richard decided to pull him up. He just didn't have enough left in the tank.

On the way home I said to Brian, 'This bad run can't continue, can it?'

'I hope not,' he replied sombrely.

So much for making the headlines in the *Racing Post*. Unless they wanted an exclusive on a once-successful horse lost in the wilderness we didn't have much to offer them. Unfortunately, I didn't need a national paper shouting the news. I had the good folk of Cefn Fforest for that. I couldn't leave the house in spring of 2008 without someone asking, 'How's Sicknote?'

Or: 'Has he got a job on Barry Beach with all the other donkeys yet?'

And, the worst: 'Are you going into the dogfood business yet?'

Comedians the lot of them, one and all.

I wouldn't have minded the ribbing if it didn't seem so deserved. To the outside, I suppose Dream really did look like he'd gone off the boil. Only on the inside did we know the mitigating circumstances. Even so, if things didn't pick up soon someone was going to get a clobbering from yours truly . . .

At least we had some good news on the horizon. Recurring Dream was at Philip's and doing nicely, although still a year away from competing. And we had another new arrival in the pipeline. Rewbell was so strong and healthy and happy we decided to have her covered one final time. You never forget your first but every new horse is exciting and Ron the vet helped us at every stage. I couldn't wait for junior to appear – as long as it got its timing right. The foal was due to be born at the start of April. If we were lucky it would be any day apart from the fifth. That was when Dream Alliance was due to return to Aintree for the Grand National support race.

'I think she'll foal before then,' Ron the vet said. 'You should be all right.'

'That's lovely,' I said. 'We've had quite enough bad luck of late. I don't think I could bear any more.'

Monday the 1st and the foal didn't come. Tuesday and Wednesday, both nothing. On Thursday I rang Ron. 'Will it be making an appearance or not? I've got a race to go to.'

'It's definitely coming today although it could be a late night.'

We were updated through the evening. At about nine o'clock we got the call to go down. Rewbell had foaled, and it was a big one. So big, in fact, Rewbell had suffered severe internal bleeding during the birth.

I was in such turmoil when we arrived. On the one hand there was our newest Ianto, a huge and healthy-looking colt. And there was his mum in obvious distress.

'Can you do anything, Ron?' Brian asked.

'I've stopped the pain but that's about it,' he said. 'I'm hoping the bleeding will stop on its own. If it doesn't . . .'

He didn't need to finish.

Despite her condition Rewbell was still a mum. She suckled that foal as if nothing had happened. We were so in admiration of her. After a few hours Ron said, 'Well, nothing's changed. You may as well get yourselves some sleep. You have a big day tomorrow.'

The race! I'd completely forgotten. On the drive home I asked Brian if he thought we should still go.

'We'll give Ron a call in the morning and if Rewbell's okay then we've got time to get up there. We've got a few hours.'

It turned out we didn't have any time at all.

We pulled into our drive and there was a fella standing at our door. It was Ron's brother.

'I'm sorry,' he said, 'Ron tried to get hold of you but

your phones are off. I'm afraid Rewbell didn't make it. She's gone.'

We hadn't even got out the car and we were hightailing it back again. It was a wordless journey. Neither of us knew what to say. When we got there and I saw Rewbell still lying next to her defenceless little boy, the floodgates opened. I never thought I'd feel that way over an animal but I swear it was like losing a member of the family. We owed everything to Rewbell. She was the real star of our allotment. The one who stayed with us, let us care for her for so many years. The one who gave us our champion.

But her last act was to give us someone else – and he needed urgent care. Without a mum, Ianto Jr wouldn't last the weekend, maybe not even the night. Foals suckle on the hour.

'He's going to require feeding from a bowl with formula. It'll make him easier to wean later,' Ron said. 'What do you want to do about that?'

'We'll be doing it ourselves, then,' Brian said. 'We'd better get home and get the horse box.'

The next morning we had to phone Howard and tell him we couldn't go. Brian suggested I went but I was too upset. For me, the horses came before the races.

'No,' I said, 'we'll watch it on the TV. We'll need something to cheer ourselves up.'

That was if we could stay awake. We had baby Ianto in a horsebox on the driveway and every hour, day and night, one of us had to go out and feed him. We took it in turns so the other could get a couple of hours' sleep or get some bits done. It was hard work. But we were happy to do it. It's what his mother would have wanted.

It's at times like this you realize you're truly a breeder, not an owner. No one else from the syndicate was working round the clock feeding a foal. That wasn't their job. But it was mine.

I was sad not to be at Aintree. I'd never missed a single race of Dream's before. What's more, after the terrible luck he'd had not finishing the last three races despite being in pole position in two of them, I really felt this day was going to be important. I suppose in the end it was, just not how I wished.

Brian had the television on and we had a chat with our daughter who'd gone up with Howard and his wife, Angela. She said he was looking good and feisty up close, just as we like him. He was showing that famous spirit, Sasha reckoned. That pleased me no end. I needed a bit of cheering. I decided I'd watch this one because it felt less scary on TV. But as 3.25 drew closer I knew I couldn't do it. As the list of runners was put up onscreen I found myself wandering over to the staircase and planting myself down.

'Are you really not going to watch?' Brian asked.

'No, I can listen to the commentary and you can tell me if I miss anything.'

'No change there then.'

The John Smith's Extra Cold Handicap Hurdle was

three miles and half a furlong. There were thirteen fences and the going was good. Dream was back up to 16/1 which gives some idea of the quality of the field. Ruby Walsh on Forest Pennant was favourite. A. P. McCoy was also heavily fancied on the future Grand National winner Don't Push It. It was a tough ask but I felt confident that, barring any more freakish occurrences, Dream could more than hold his own.

They set off and I could quickly tell that Richard Johnson and Dream Alliance were back in the groove. It was weird having only Brian's shouting and swearing to keep me company but I managed to tune him out enough to hear the TV commentary. Dream seemed to be doing all right, challenging the other riders more with every jump, and by the halfway mark he was taking the fight to the leaders.

Brian was going nuts. 'He's going to win it. I swear he's going to bloody win it.'

I tell you now, sitting on the stairs hugging your knees in your own house is a damn sight more stressful than pacing around an owners' enclosure. Being so far away, I felt I couldn't do anything to help our boy – not that I could normally. It just always felt important that we were there, if only so I could tell him I loved him and repeat my promise that if he did his best he was coming home with me at the end of his career. Him in Liverpool and me in Wales was killing me.

They were approaching the ninth and Brian was getting super animated. Suddenly it changed.

'Oh no,' he said suddenly. 'He's gone down.'

It took a second for the words to be processed in my brain. Then I was up off my backside and running round to the telly.

'What happened? What did you see?'

'He made the jump but he landed bad and went over. That's all I saw.'

Of course the television people still had a race to cover so we were in the dark. I jumped on the phone to Sasha. No answer. I tried Howard. Nothing. I kept ringing, ping-ponging between them, but no one picked up. I was going out of my mind.

A couple of minutes later the race ended and the cameras focused once again on the ninth fence. It was empty apart from a tent being erected behind the jump.

'Oh Christ,' Brian said, 'oh no.'

'What is it?' I said. 'What's wrong?'

But we were both staring at the same television. I knew the answer as well as him. Screens being put up around a fallen horse only ever meant one thing.

'They're going to shoot him, Brian, aren't they? They're going to shoot our boy.'

He couldn't answer through the tears.

16

If There is Anything You Can Do

After the night we'd had with Rewbell and Ianto I was broken already. I didn't think I had another tear to shed. But I found some all right. You feel such a fool standing there in daylight in your sitting room sobbing at the TV. But what choice did we have? Our pride and joy was about to be euthanized by a vet. It was like losing a child.

I was vaguely aware of the phone ringing. I ignored it for a while. I didn't want to talk to anyone. Finally I answered. It was Howard.

'I've been trying to get hold of you and Sasha,' I said. 'Why didn't you answer?'

'Jan, I'm so sorry. Neither of us knew what to say.'

'Have they done it?' I asked. 'Have they ended him?'

'That's why I'm calling: no. Richard wouldn't let them.'

'Oh, thank the lord.'

Over the course of the next few hours a fuller picture emerged. Coming up to the jump Richard noticed that one of the hurdles was down, damaged by another horse. Dream managed to dodge it but in doing so his legs concertinaed and he cut himself. The shoes the horses wear are like razors, so when the back leg caught the front leg it sliced through.

The course vet suspected it had gone through the tendon. Dream was in great pain just standing up. The screens were erected as per procedure. The next step was a no-brainer.

But Richard wouldn't let it happen.

A lot of owners don't really know their own horses. They buy them and sell them and, at the end of the day, they are viewed as assets. Like a computer or a lorry. The harsh reality is, there's no insurance money for an injured racehorse. But if it dies that's another story and they will pay out. Richard knew that Dream was more than money to us.

He said to the vet, 'If there is anything else you can do, do not put him down. These are not your average owners. They will not want that.'

I won't ever forget Richard for doing that. He saved our Dream.

The Institute of Veterinary Science in Liverpool is where they train the vets of the future. If anyone could help us, the vet said, it was them.

They confirmed Dream had severed his own tendon. They were able to fix the wound but not the internal problem. When Howard rang the next day it was to say, 'The fantastic news is Dream's going to live. But he'll never run again.'

I still remember the sadness in his voice. He thought that was his lost youth disappearing again, I could hear it.

I can't call him out for being selfish, though, can I? Because what was I thinking? *Oh, Dream, I'm so sorry, love. But at least now you can come back home to me where you belong.* It didn't matter that Brian and I were hand-rearing a foal on the hour every hour on our driveway. It would take more than that to stop me wanting to care for my boy.

That's how we left it. We'd wind the syndicate down, Dream would come back to us and life would move on. Brian and I would get Ianto up and running and soon enough Recurring Dream would make her debut.

Then Philip ruined all that.

He rang Howard to say he'd spoken to the institute himself and they'd discussed an experimental new treatment involving stem cell surgery. The vets reckoned it stood a very good chance of working for Dream's injury – did we want Philip to look into it?

Of course, Howard said yes.

It turns out it had been done a couple of times before but while the horses involved significantly improved in strength they never achieved anything on the track again. The other issue was more straightforward.

'It's very expensive,' Philip said. 'Probably around £20,000.'

If I'd had the money I'd have slapped it in his hands as soon as possible. However much I wanted my boy home, I wanted him to fulfil his destiny more. Dream loved racing, I knew that. And he loved pleasing us. I thought, *We have to give him a chance.* I didn't have the cash to pay for the operation but I knew someone who did.

Dream Alliance.

If you think about it, all the winnings he'd earned over the years were sitting there in a bank account with his name on it. The master plan was that at the end of his career we'd divvy up the balance and each syndicate member would get a tidy sum. Now, that was what was agreed in the syndicate constitution.

'But what,' I said to Howard, 'if we let Dream pay for his own treatment instead?'

'All I can do is put it to the syndicate,' he said. 'Do you think they'll go for it?'

'I don't know. The number of members who've had a problem with me or you over the years, they could vote against it out of spite, I suppose.'

'Yes,' he said. 'Then you've got the ones who ask me after every race to divide the winnings now. I don't think they'll be happy seeing their nest egg being dipped into.'

It was a pretty miserable conversation to be honest. But we had to ask them, didn't we? We owed it to Dream to give them a chance to save him.

Howard called a meeting up at the club and laid it all out as fairly and honestly as he could. He explained how this revolutionary new treatment could significantly improve Dream's quality of life. There were no guarantees that he would ever race again and certainly no promise that he would ever scale the same heights as before, but he would be better for it.

He went through the finances and pointed out that no one would have to put their hand in their pocket. It would all be covered by Dream's own winnings. But, he said, 'You all have a claim to that money so it has to be a unanimous vote.'

He concluded by saying, 'Philip Hobbs thinks it's worth a try. And for what it's worth, so do I. We've had a great run and I think we owe it to the horse to try everything. So personally, I'll be voting for yes.'

'So will I,' said Brian. And, you know what, he wasn't alone. One by one every single member of the syndicate voted to spend the money to save the horse.

Their horse.

Perhaps that was the first time I ever let myself admit he had never really been mine.

Dream was taken down to London and stem cells were removed from his sternum and then developed in a petri dish. It's the realm of science fiction really, and to think it was being done for a horse. At that stage you have to commit to just letting the experts do what they do, but when we were told the stem cells had become contaminated and unusable I did wonder whether it was all too much of a fantasy.

There was a bit of negotiation and we agreed they'd try again for half price. This time it was successful. The cells grew enough in the dish to be injected into Dream's injured leg. After that it was a waiting game.

This all happened within a week of Aintree and the accident in April 2008. Even without the sleep deprivation from looking after Ianto twenty-four-seven, I think it still would have been a blur. After the surgery, Dream was moved down to Philip's to recuperate and I was straight over. I'd like to say he looked fantastic but it wouldn't be true. He seemed really poorly, really sorry for himself. All four legs were bandaged to prevent him favouring one leg over another. It's a trick vets use to make horses think they're okay, but it made him look worse physically than he was.

'I'm sorry it's been scary,' I said to him, 'but we're trying to help you all we can.'

I know we were paying, but Philip could easily have said, 'This isn't worth our time and effort. We're not nurses.' He didn't. In fact, the whole team was brilliant. Our boy didn't want for anything and I think it paid off. Each time I visited I could see an improvement. Then one day Johnson said, 'We walked him today.' He was as excited as I was. After that things got better and better. This experimental treatment appeared to be working.

Whether it would be enough to get Dream back to his rightful place on the track was another question.

I wish I could say that Dream was the only concern at that time but the truth was my father was ill. We hadn't always had the best relationship but that's the adult in me talking. As a kid I'd had no complaints at all. He'd been a good father when I was young. I wouldn't have achieved anything without him, I reckon. He had a good idea of right and wrong and of course he showed me how to be a breeder with his budgerigars. I don't suppose he meant to set me down this competitive path, but he did.

Over the years, he had come to accept Brian as my husband. Any bad feeling between them faded away and Brian helped to look after him as his illness got worse. On 9 March 2009, with my dad lying in a hospital bed having been bedridden for years, we both went to visit him. My mother was in a wheelchair next to the bed and I chatted away while Brian stood looking out the window. After about half an hour my dad said, 'Janet, my love, would you mind if I had a word with your Brian?'

Of course I didn't mind. He trusted Brian and knew he would take care of our family when he was gone. That meant a lot to me. He died shortly after, but not before wishing me the best of luck with Dream. He'd loved being called after every race and had lived a whole new life through me. Breeding winners was still in his heart and I'm happy he died knowing Dream was going to be all right.

*

It must have been six months down the line from Dream's injury when we got a call to visit Sandhill. They were going to take our boy out onto the gallops for the first time. It was going to be a landmark day. Either Dream would get round and we'd have him back in the game or he'd falter and we'd know the racing was over. Whichever way, there was going to be a conclusion by the end of the day.

Brian and I went down there with Howard and we stood against the rail as we'd done so many times before. It reminded me of the old days when we didn't know what kind of a horse we had on our hands. The nervous anticipation was the same. The only difference now was, five years later, we knew exactly what kind of animal we had: a fighter. Now it was up to him to prove it.

We could see the horses in the distance. They were swinging round and heading towards us. The yard jockeys don't wear our colours of course, but I didn't need them to spot our boy. As they got closer I felt the goosebumps on my arms. He was doing it, he was running, he wasn't giving up on us.

The sound of hooves pounding the earth is something you don't always hear at the racetracks above the noise of the crowd. But we could hear it now. Thudding and thudding and thudding, louder and louder and louder, and suddenly they were past and gone. I was speechless. Brian was speechless. Howard was grinning.

'Did you see that?' he said. 'Dream winked at us.'

'Oh, come on, Howard, don't be daft.'

'No, I swear as I'm standing here. He winked as he went by. He's giving us a message. He's telling us he's okay.'

It was a day for bold claims. When we went down to the stables afterwards Brian had a good look at Dream and said, 'He will definitely race again. And, you know what? He will win.'

I always listen to my husband where horses are concerned. But this was a heck of a claim. I didn't want to get my hopes up again.

Naturally Philip was less gung-ho but a few weeks later he declared Dream ready to train again.

'See,' Brian said. 'I'm not wrong.'

Finally the light at the end of the tunnel. It's Bath Race Course, 31 July 2009. It's the culmination of a long journey. I can't wait for the race to get going. Everything we've been working towards is out there right now. The race begins and I quickly realize we're not in competition. We're at the back and in no danger of doing any better. The commentator confirms it.

'And in ninth place, trained by Philip Hobbs – it's Recurring Dream.'

I hoped the distraction of his sister's fledgling career would help me through Dream's own return. Unfortunately, after two disappointing races Philip admitted he just didn't see anything there. He didn't want to take our money if he personally didn't believe in the project. That wasn't to say another trainer couldn't get anything out of her. John Flint agreed to have her back and see how she went. Sadly, another three races just confirmed Philip's opinion.

While Recurring's own syndicate took care of the bills during her short career, I decided to go down a different route with Ianto. I wanted to fund him myself and see how far that got us. He'd already had my sleep for six months, what was a bit of money after that?

After a fortnight on the driveway, Ianto had been taken up to the allotment. We were backwards and forwards, backwards and forwards. By then he only needed feeding every two hours. During the day Brian and I shared it, alternating. At night he wouldn't let me go up there because there were no lights.

Ianto was so fragile and lonely without his mother the temptation was to go in and play with him and pet him but all the advice from our trainer friends said not to. It's bad enough he was being hand-reared, they said. If we started treating him like a domestic animal he'd have no fear of people and we wouldn't get any work from him.

Okay, we thought, *what can we do for him instead?*

We decided the next best thing would be another horse. Because he was so young we didn't want anything too big in case he got hurt so we got him a little Shetland pony called Shadow as a stable mate. I can't tell you how much of a mistake that was. The pony pasted Ianto and he nearly killed him. He was nasty, he rammed him, head-butted him and bit the back of his neck. Classic small horse syndrome. He was a bully, he was a vandal. We stuck it for a few months then we had to get rid of Shadow.

His social life was suffering but at least Ianto had decent digs. On the night before the Hennessy in 2007 we had terrible high winds and rain. Brian had gone up to feed Rewbell in the morning and discovered the corrugated iron roof curled up like a salmon's tail. He had to climb up there and flatten it down but he's not one of the world's great DIYers. Give him an animal and he will bring it back from the dead. Ask him to hang a picture and he will knock in a 6-inch nail. To be fair, he'd originally built the stable himself but it was a ramshackle affair. It couldn't take much more patching. When I saw the bodge job on the roof I said, 'I think it's time to admit we need proper facilities.'

We hadn't touched my breeder's prize money so it seemed sensible to dip into it for this. Looking at the result, £1,500 later, I hoped we'd done the right thing.

With horses, though, you're never far away from the next unexpected bill so I decided to take on another job. It had to fit in with everything else so when I heard the big ASDA round the way needed someone to clean its tills from 4 a.m. to 8 a.m. I took it up. I'll be honest, I expected it to be a bit of a chore, but there's humour in everything. Because it's open twenty-four hours you get all sorts come in. One morning, really early on, we had a drag artist come in in all his stage regalia. He walked through the doors and said, 'Don't ask!'

I wasn't the only one struggling for money. Christine Brunnock had been a staunch supporter of Dream since the beginning. But she came to me during Dream's layoff and said, 'I'm sorry, Jan, but I can't keep going with the syndicate. I have to make some savings and that £40 a month could really make a difference.'

'Christine, don't be silly. You've been here so long. You're owed a slice of the pie – you won't get anything if you walk away now.'

'I know,' she said, 'but I feel guilty not contributing any more so you can use my share to make up the difference.'

I tried and tried to persuade her to stay. I said there were great times to come. Anything that came into my head.

'Jan, I wish that were true. But there are no guarantees Dream will race again, let alone compete for prizes.'

'All the more reason to stay! You'll get your payout as soon as he retires. If you reckon it's sooner rather than later you're quids in.'

'No, I'm sorry,' she said. 'My mind's made up. I just wish I weren't leaving you all in the lurch.'

I was so sad to see her go. There were one or two others in the syndicate who I could have waved goodbye to without a second thought, but Christine was a good one and I was sorry it was her finances that drove her decision. Although she rarely came to races because she didn't enjoy the atmosphere she never wavered in voting in Dream's best interests.

I didn't show it to her but Christine's decision to walk away knocked my confidence a little.

That night I confided in Brian with all my worries. 'Do you think we're mad carrying on?' I said. 'You know, after everything.'

'What do you think?' he asked.

'Personally I think Dream's best is yet to come. In fact, if you ask me, greatness is just around the corner.'

'There's only one way to find out,' he said. 'He has to run again.'

And boy, he did.

17

He's in the Effin' Lead

A little white spot.

That tiny little blemish was the only reminder of the hell Dream Alliance had endured eighteen months earlier. It's amazing to see how such a savage wound and the results of some highly invasive surgery were almost invisible a year and a half later. To the untrained eye he'd obviously made a full recovery. But had he? Only time would tell – and that time was 3.15 p.m. on 4 November 2009.

The WBX.COM Handicap Hurdle at Chepstow was a calculated gentle entry back into the world of racing. For a start it wasn't the terrifying fences and ditches of the steeplechase but the less demanding hurdles. It was also only over two miles and seven-and-a-half furlongs, with just twelve obstacles to negotiate. In other words, Philip was easing my boy back in.

I've never had a harsh word to say about Philip but he had a lot riding on this one. Physically, he swore that

Dream had made a full recovery. Watching him going full pelt on the gallops you'd believe those eighteen months might not ever have happened. But they had, and we had the £20,000 bill to prove it. It was psychologically that Dream could have a problem, Philip said. Apparently there was a type of PTSD with horses and that could take more time to heal. We said it was up to him when Dream should re-enter the fray and he picked Chepstow.

Let's hope you're right, lad.

Philip wasn't the only one making impossible decisions. In the run-up to Dream's return, Howard, Derek and Brian had to have a difficult conversation with Philip. They prefaced it all by saying how grateful we were to Richard Johnson for keeping our horse alive at Aintree. That was a debt that could never be repaid. However, the series of races prior to that, and including it, I suppose, hadn't gone well for Dream or Richard. Without any hint of blame, we all thought it was time for a change of jockey. I'm not particularly superstitious but it felt like at some point the combination of Richard and Dream together must have galloped over a black cat or on a broken mirror under a ladder. The amount of bad luck they'd had was just obscene. We owed it to the syndicate to try to change it. We were, after all, the guardians of their money and their trust.

'It can't be doing Richard's reputation any good having four non-finishes in a row,' Howard said. 'No one is to blame. We just have to be seen to be being pro-active for our members. We're a syndicate, not a dictatorship.'

Philip, to his credit, said he'd honour the request. And so we were introduced to Giles Hawkins. He was nice enough and incredibly positive about Dream's chances in a field that included several decent mounts. Usually that would be enough to satisfy any owner but after our recent run of terrible luck Brian said, 'I hope he's wearing a rabbit's foot or we're going to look silly.' Philip was more practical. He just told Giles to let the horse enjoy the race. 'He needs to feel part of things again.'

Although Christine Brunnock never came to races, once the 3.15 came round and the starting rope dropped, I was suddenly aware of her absence from the group. In my mind I thought whatever happened that day could be dedicated to her.

I also felt the keen absence of my father. As well as visiting the graves of Brian's parents en route, as was tradition, we also stopped by Dad for me to keep him up to date. It was hard but I found the words. I just hoped he heard them.

As well as being hurdles, the race was a handicap. As befitted his 8/1 standing, Dream was given eleven stone to carry. I couldn't understand where they got either figure from. The lad hadn't raced for eighteenth months. Did the bookies know something we didn't? Did they have a spy at Minehead?

Mr Mackay with Warren Marston in the saddle got

away first. Passato and Sarde quickly filled in second and third positions. Giles got Dream Alliance nestled at fifth which was perfect in my book. Before the second jump the top three positions had changed but Dream stayed where he was. Passato snatched the lead before the second and Cannon Fire suddenly appeared in the mix. Boomerang and Dance Island were in and around.

It was one of those races where the top six or seven were fluid. A mile and four hurdles in we had Dream in third behind Mr Mackay and Passato. The commentator was calling it with no emotion. We had enough for everyone.

Approaching halfway and entering the back straight to take hurdles six, seven and eight, Dream was holding on to third. The front two were jostling away and Sarde started coming up on the inside of Dream.

He won't like that, I thought.

There wasn't much he could do. Dream was down to fourth and then fifth with four more hurdles to take. The track commentator had him fading. I didn't believe it. Not after what I'd seen on the gallops. Coming into the straight it was Passato, Mr Mackay, Silver Spinner and Dream Alliance in that order. Three to jump and Dream suddenly got going but Dance Island got going even more. He came tearing round the outside, effortlessly taking the lead. As the others wilted the only horse keeping up was Dream Alliance.

As they came over the second to last it was just Dream

and Dance Island. By the last they were five or six lengths ahead of the chasing pack and in the end the horse carrying almost a stone less than our boy, Dance Island, crossed the winning post first. After the tendon split, the experimental surgery, the eighteen-month layoff and the general bad luck of the last two years, we had to be very, very happy with that.

Not only had he proved himself physically very capable, Dream also appeared over two miles and seven furlongs to banish any demons from his mind. There was a very real prospect that he'd flinch at the memory of being hurt over a jump and pull up or unseat Giles. But he didn't. He was strong. He took every obstacle in his stride. Literally. His psychological healing was as advanced as his physical if not more so.

Philip was always my litmus test and he was over the moon with second. As usual, in the same breath that he complimented us and the horse he also broached the subject of the next race.

'You've got the Hennessy coming again or another crack at the Welsh National. Considering the likely fields, I recommend the latter.'

I don't know whether it was a result of the huge financial investment they'd all made or just the shot in the arm of Dream running again after a year and a half, but that choice – one which customarily would have been made between Philip, Howard and me – found itself being discussed at syndicate level.

There were passionate arguments for each. Some wanted to go to the Hennessy because not only had it been a fabulous day out last time but Dream had also come second. Others said that the threat of meeting Denman again meant the same result at best whereas the Welsh had a new field of horses Dream could challenge. The third view was that of the superstitious: Dream had failed once at the Welsh. Why risk it again?

Howard took the same view as Philip. 'Because of the way they calculate the weights at the Hennessey, Dream would be carrying less at the Welsh Grand National than he would at the Gold Cup. That has to influence his chances and therefore, I suggest, our decision.'

It proved the persuasive argument. It was agreed. We were going again to the Welsh.

Giles Hawkins had done a top job for us but for the 2009 Welsh Grand National Philip decided Tom O'Brien had to get the ride. He knew the horse and, more importantly some might say, he knew us.

Once again, a phalanx of Welshmen and -women descended upon Chepstow. I was honoured to be among them. As I told my dad when I'd laid flowers on his plot earlier, I truly believed Dream had a chance.

In the parade ring he looked good. His eyes were shining, his coat was gleaming and his physique was a work of art. If I hadn't already put money on him I would have done then. We had a chat with Tom then retreated to a cosy spot on the rails by the parade ring. It's not the best view if I'm honest, it's quite low, but considering I'd only be listening to the race that didn't bother me unduly.

The race itself – the Coral Welsh National Handicap Chase – was three miles and five furlongs. The going was said to be heavy and two of the prescribed twenty fences were omitted. Dream was down to carry 10s 8lbs. At least another seven horses were lugging more. How the various weights were worked out was a mystery to me given the tons we'd had to carry recently. All I can say is we were grateful for a fairer distribution for once.

As 2.10 approached everyone started to calm down. Most of the syndicate was with us, plus their families. Whether they'd voted for this race or the Hennessy, they were determined to back their boy. That was fabulous. At some level I believed Dream could feel the support.

Looking at the race card, Le Beau Bai was the biggest threat. At 4/1 he was the favourite. A shade behind at 5/1 was The Tother One ridden by the inimitable A. P. McCoy, champion jockey supreme. Operation Houdini was 8/1, Old Benny, Halcon Genelardais and Coe 10/1, Silver By Nature and Flintoff 14/1, Gone To Lunch and Ballyfitz 16/1 and Nozic 18/1. Even Kornati Kid, a friendly face from Philip's stable and ridden by our friend Richard Johnson, was 14/1. In fact, at 20/1 ourselves, there were only five horses rated with lower chances than Dream Alliance. As usual, I assumed the bookies knew what they were doing. And, as usual, Brian was rubbing his hands.

'We're getting a slap-up meal out of this race I can tell you,' he promised. '20/1? I could run it and have those odds. Dream's going to clean up today and no mistake.'

Of course he was being the proud father, but he'd also seen Dream close up in the parade ring and in the stables earlier. In his mind there was no doubt. Dream would be top three minimum. With £40 at 20/1 each way that was more than a meal. That was a holiday.

If, that is, Dream placed. While Brian was confident, I wasn't so sure. I'd been looking at Dream's track record and felt I was beginning to understand the pattern. Every time in the past that Dream Alliance had endured a hard race, he'd drifted away for a few months following it. It had happened after Exeter and again after going up against Denman at the Hennessy. I didn't believe it was psychological, there was obviously something physio-logical that he overextended on those occasions. I just didn't know what. Nor, sadly, did the experts.

I watched the horses gather for the start. Richard had a bit of bother corralling Kornati Kid into line and a trainer ran over but as soon as he did the rope dropped and they were off.

Flintoff and Hello Bud, a 28/1 runner, set off first. Dream took fourth, perfect. They climbed the hill for the first time. At the first of the twenty fences, Hello Bud went over, with everyone following safely. Dream was down to sixth by the second hurdle. Towards the fourth and Flintoff made a mistake. A long run before the seventh. Two lengths separated Kilbeggan Blade, Hello Bud and Coe from Mio De Beauchene and my boy, Dream Alliance. He was making ground. Fabulous.

When you're listening you only have the pictures in your mind to match the words. Hearing Dream back in fifth didn't trouble me. There'd been that much movement already I was confident either he or Tom had a plan. Some of those ahead were showing their hands too early. Of that I was convinced. The question at a third of the distance was, could Dream close the gap in time?

Coming up to the second of the ditches I had everything clenched. Dream had never had a problem with the water jumps but as a punter looking at them, I couldn't see how any of the horses got over. They couldn't see what was on the other side. Was it just luck? Based on Dream's fortunes for the last two years you can understand why I was on tenterhooks.

Over jump ten – the halfway stage – and all eighteen runners were upright and pointing in the right direction, and with jockeys on their backs. Moments later the commentary was in danger of being drowned out as the stars of the show passed by the stands. I admit, I took a peep. It was all over so quickly I can't even say for sure whether I saw Dream or not. But I saw the pack and he, according to the tannoy, was towards the front of it.

Approaching the eleventh Dream was fourth, back in

the hot seat, back where I'd have put him if you'd given me a choice.

Watching the pack is almost poetic. Their strides are approximately in tandem. And regardless of the width of the track they all bunch together like a shoal of fish chasing smaller food. From above they're a brown mass moving as one. As beautiful as it was, I realized I couldn't stand the pressure and turned my back again. As I started pacing up and down the stands once more I noticed Howard doing the same thing. Silly pair of fools. As if we could influence anything from where we were. But clearly we both thought we'd try.

No more than fifteen lengths separated the whole field as they surmounted fence eleven. At number twelve, an open ditch, the leader Hello Bud was outjumped by Coe. Even though it wasn't my horse I clenched my fist. The front runners were going to wear themselves out fighting each other. That was my prediction. That was my hope.

Even as I thought it, the commentator announced that Hello Bud had slipped to third behind ours truly.

Now we've got them.

As the pack jumped for the last time on the far side of the course, Miko De Beauchene was on the outside and challenging. All three horses were within a length and a bit. Hello Bud had said goodbye.

Around the long left-hand bend they straightened towards the fourth last. The front runners cleared but behind the news wasn't so good. Operation Houdini went over, taking Hello Bud with him.

The noise from our section of the owners' enclosure was nearing nuclear.

'What's going on?' I asked Brian.

He didn't answer.

'Brian!' I shouted.

He might not admit it now but he swore at me to leave him alone. In doing so, he mentioned that Dream was pulling level with Coe. They were eyeball to eyeball. I'd looked into our horse's eyes barely twenty minutes earlier. They were full of passion and concentration. For that reason alone I knew what was coming. *Coe doesn't stand a chance.*

I also knew I had to witness it happen for myself.

For the first time in our relationship I watched from afar as my boy outpsyched his rival and inched ahead. The next jump and I leapt into the air higher than he did, I reckon. I didn't need the commentator to tell me that Coe had made a mistake. Of course he had! You don't play mind games with our boy. I swear, Dream didn't break Coe physically, it was mental. He just wasn't prepared to be beaten.

'Brian,' I said.

'Yes,' he replied, 'he's in the effin' lead.'

So that cleared that up.

We still had to get home, mind. At the second last Silver By Nature had come up to challenge. He was good.

He was close. But as they landed, Dream was a length ahead. As they cleared the last, a gasp went up from everyone related to the syndicate. Dream had stumbled on landing but he was okay.

The push to the end was brutal. It was mesmerizing and tortuous at the same time. As Dream Alliance pounded towards the finish, Silver By Nature was hoovering up our five lengths lead. I had every faith in Tom O'Brien but from the outside it was horrible. Another few yards and I felt we'd have been second. But, in fact, we weren't. We weren't second at all. Not even close. We were first.

Dream Alliance had won the Welsh Grand National.

I honestly didn't know what to do with myself. The first thing I thought of was to get out my phone and dial a familiar number. It rang half a dozen times before I thought, *Oh, he's not going to answer.*

Out of habit I'd phoned my dad.

I was that proud I'd just wanted to speak to him. It was an amazing feeling. After nineteen months, half of it fighting for his mobility, Dream Alliance had won one of the top races in the National Hunt calendar. And he'd done it for Wales. I could not have wished for anything more. Even the Hennessy would not have compared to this.

Everyone took the win in different ways. Brian was a jumping bean. People were hugging and kissing and a few were crying. Everything was in slow motion. It was like being in a bubble. I was a spectator in my own body and mind. Things just seemed to happen. I wasn't fully aware of being involved.

As we made our way to the winner's enclosure the commentator continued his work. A fairytale return from injury, he said. And he was right. Two years earlier our boy had pulled up in the same race. A year after that he was in bandages. But today, on the day that mattered, on the day that the hopes of the whole syndicate and all of Cefn Fforest were on him, Dream Alliance showed the class he'd always had. And we were about to thank him.

At Sandhill Philip ran such a tight ship, but in the wild, as it were, he had to accept certain people would try to introduce alien elements into his charges' diets. So when we offered Dream carrots and Polo mints, there was nothing to be said. We just wanted our boy to know we were so happy with him. In fact, beyond happy. We were proud. Through him we'd achieved something in our lives.

Watching Dream parade around in the frost, his chestnut coat appearing almost tan in the winter half-light, I wondered if I'd ever been happier. Going up to collect the £57,010 cheque for winning and the substantially smaller one for breeding didn't top that initial sensation. Not even the beautiful gold trophy they handed me could. Yes, we danced with it and paraded with it and passed it around but it was superficial in a way. There was something inside me that was singing so loud it didn't need accompaniment. And it was this: I'd set out to produce a thoroughbred champion racer and, you'd have to say, I, Janet Vokes, had done it.

End of story.

18

I Can't Watch this Torture Any More

No one was calling him a donkey now.

The mood in Cefn Fforest was sensational. It reminded me of how everyone got the trestle tables out for the Queen's Silver Jubilee in 1977. There weren't quite parties in the street after Dream Alliance won the Welsh Grand National, but everyone had a smile – apart from some of the gamblers, that is. So many people in the village put a bet on Dream winning that the local bookmakers ran out of money. They only keep so much cash in the shops, they said, and it was a week before some people could collect their winnings.

For days it took me an hour to get anywhere. People wanted to have a chat and tell me what they were doing, where they watched the race, how much they'd won, how they'd always supported Dream, how they'd never doubted him even during his wilderness times. In the years since I think a few wires have been crossed in the memories. The amount of people today who say they were at Chepstow to the see 'their boy' win in the flesh would fill the course six times over. But you can't help but be happy. Any chance to bring a community together and you have to take it.

That community spirit was particularly prominent in the syndicate. After all that time and the various things that had been said, I couldn't call too many of them close friends any more, but in the immediate afterglow of the Welsh none of that mattered. As we were getting ready to leave the course Howard had said, 'We need to go and celebrate.' It was completely spontaneous and everyone said yes. No one wanted the party mood to end. We went to the Halfway pub in Wiley, near Blackwood, and ordered steak and chips for thirty with drinks to keep flowing. It was great, actually. Everyone relived the race in their own words. I didn't have much to contribute, having had my back to the action for most of it. But seeing how their faces lit up talking about it warmed me inside. Possibly for the first time I could see with my own eyes what my daft old ambition had done for so many others. When I started out the syndicate was a means to an end. I needed their money straight and simple. After so much water under the bridge I needed reminding sometimes that these investors had given more than their money. They'd given their hearts and souls as well, just like me.

One of the joys of the Halfway is that because it's in a bit of a dip, you don't get a mobile signal. I can't tell you how much of a pleasure it is to be in a pub without every other person on their phone. It was no different this day. When we got out to the cars, mind, a bit of signal creeped through and our phones went crazy. Everyone had messages, missed calls, you name it, from everyone they knew. It was the first sign that Dream's achievements were making waves.

Not every call was from friends and family though. I couldn't believe it when I was trawling through my voicemails on the drive home and I got one from a complete stranger.

'Well, that's odd,' I said to Brian.

'Who was it?' he asked.

'It was a lady from Sky News. They want to interview me.'

'Oh,' he said. 'We'd better get the kettle on then.'

That was only the start of it. The Sky people came over with their cameras and their microphones and they interviewed me and Brian and Howard and we took them to the allotment and they recorded everything. The BBC weren't far behind. Then the newspaper journalists and the freelance photographers started ringing and booking appointments. Some just turned up on the doorstep, drenched in rain more often than not. And they all wanted to know the same thing.

'How did you do it? How did you raise a horse on an allotment on a slag heap in Wales and turn him into a champion?'

It didn't stop there. Because I'm on Facebook and other social media, we had people message us from Australia, New Zealand, America, all over the world, saying, 'I've just seen this on Sky telly and I want to tell you I think it's amazing what you've done for yourself and the area.'

Closer to home the phone started ringing off the hook with friends and family and acquaintances from the past. People we knew up in west Wales, people we'd worked with and fallen out of contact with, distant relatives – they all found the time to dig out our number and say 'well done'. They said, 'We've seen you on the TV, we've seen you in the magazines and newspapers and heard you on the radio, we're so proud.'

It was the start of something very different in my life but not something unpleasant. After so many years fighting for my own identity, to have these massive media outlets chase after me was flattering in a way I can't really explain. Like I say, I'm comfortable in my own skin. Having Dream win the Welsh was all the acknowledgement I needed that I had succeeded in my goals. The rest was just flim-flam – but it was nice, I won't lie to you. Not a single caption on the news or in the papers mentioned Kelly, Trevor or Daisy. They just said two words: Janet Vokes.

A massive part of the story, of course, is the fact it's not a one-woman success. Syndicates in racing aren't uncommon but ours was a bit unusual. The fact it was predominantly such a small community pulling together for a shared goal made it stand out. That we only had one horse as well was a bit different. But there were others beyond the syndicate who'd played a leading role in the tale.

With everything kicking off media-wise, I'm embarrassed to say it took us a week to get down to see Philip to properly thank him. But when we did, we did it en masse. The entire syndicate, I think, travelled down to Minehead the Sunday after the win and we all had our photos taken with Dream at Sandhill. I swear that boy loves a camera. You'll never see a bad picture of him. Then we treated Philip and Sarah to a lovely roast at one of his favourite local restaurants. Philip has been in the business a long time, he's had many winners and seen it all – or so he thought. As he pointed out, he'd never seen anything quite like us.

I decided to take that as a compliment.

The trophy they handed us at the Welsh was a beautiful thing and obviously very valuable. You get to pose with it, wave it around and then you hand it back. Backstage they give you a replica which, to the untrained eye, is identical – just clearly a shilling or two less expensive. For a week it went everywhere with me, including that lunch with Philip. It's still in my house, pride of place. Any member of the syndicate can borrow it whenever they want but I'm considered the custodian. All these years later I can't see it without the emotions of the win washing back over me like it was yesterday.

It wasn't just UK media that was interested. A TV crew flew over from Germany to cover the Dream Alliance story. They've been back a dozen times just to do follow ups. They've been wonderful.

It was hard to imagine our little adventure making such big waves but everywhere I went I was reminded of it. The few people in the district who didn't claim to be at Chepstow still felt involved. The mass media saturation of our story kept everyone wrapped up in it and brought us together as a community. Even if they only saw him on the television, they all felt part of the story and that, after decades of being ignored as a region, was important. Whatever their role in Dream's rise to glory, however small their part, the fact the world was looking at us made everyone stand just that little bit taller. It was never something I set out to do but I'm very proud it happened. We needed it. We deserved it.

But, like I say, every coin has two sides. For that brief period around New Year we were up, no question. The downside of the whole media circus was the expectation that Dream's success would continue.

There's a phrase: 'Those who cannot learn from history are doomed to repeat it.'

As we moved into 2010 I had the sickening feeling that would be us. Looking back over his record, I could see that though Dream had achieved many wonderful things, they'd always been followed by extended periods of non-achievement. I'm not a gambler, I wasn't his owner, but I am his breeder. I look for patterns in things. I'm always searching for ways to improve. So it was no surprise to me when Dream turned out at Haydock Park on 20 February 2010 and spectacularly failed to set the place alight.

Someone with thinner skin than me would have been embarrassed. I don't think Haydock has ever had so much outside media interest. There were that many journalists there to witness the Dream miracle they probably doubled their takings at the bar. It's such a shame they all went away without the story they'd come for.

The nice thing about the Blue Square Gold Cup Chase was that it reunited Dream with a lot of the horses he'd beaten at Chepstow. I don't know if they recognize each other but being surrounded by competitors he'd bested couldn't hurt, could it? Ballyfitz, Coe, Hello Bud, Miko De Beauchene and Silver By Nature were all there. If you were just looking at the card you'd think he'd beat them all.

It was the strangely familiar tale of Dream taking off with the pack and just not seeming to care. People say horses do what the jockey tells them but Dream was never like that. He had days when he could conquer worlds and other days when getting out of bed seemed like too much effort. Haydock Park was definitely the latter.

The commentary told me everything and nothing. It was two minutes in before I even heard Dream's name mentioned, and they don't ignore you if you're troubling the front runners. The noise from Brian et al. confirmed my fears. *This isn't the race for us.*

As it ploughed on and Dream remained conspicuous by his absence from the action, I didn't give one moment's thought to the media attention trained on the race. I spent the rest of the race thinking, *Just get round in one piece and we'll get you home. There's always tomorrow.* I think Tom the jockey was thinking the same thing. There were twenty fences and he pulled Dream up at the sixteenth. Oscar Park had fallen and our boy got rattled. There was no point in continuing. Sometimes you just have to listen to the horse.

Afterwards Tom said, 'There was nothing in the tank. I didn't want to hurt him.'

'Thank you, Tom,' I said. 'You did the right thing.'

No one believed me about the 'wilderness' pattern. They do now, mind. But at the time, when you're in the heart of the hurricane, you don't always analyse everything as clear-headedly as you might. Despite the no-show of the real Dream at Haydock he was still considered a decent bet for his next race. This wasn't some gentle hurdles event to get his dander up. This was serious. This was the big time.

This was the Grand National.

It wasn't till April so even the pessimists among us –

me included – felt he would be all right. Whatever made Dream go slowly immediately after a big win should be out of his system by the time we reached Aintree. Even so, going back to the venue where he'd nearly lost his life was a big psychological undertaking for me, if not the horse. I told myself it was nothing, a superstition, but something at the back of my mind kept saying that Aintree wasn't the course for us.

Come 10 April and an unseasonably hot day, we were once again surrounded by familiar faces. Nozic was there, Flintoff was there, Ballyfitz, Snowy Morning, Character Building, Hello Bud, Silver By Nature and Don't Push It – they were all there. And so was our boy. The only question was: which Dream would turn up? The determined fighter or the couldn't-care-less trotter?

We found out soon enough. From the off Dream wasn't involved. He stayed with the pack but definitely to the rear. It wasn't where Tom or I or Dream himself would be comfortable contending the win. It wasn't a complete shock. The hard ground didn't suit him, I knew that, and the mysterious appearance of the sun couldn't be helping either. *Still*, I thought, *if he wants to win he will.*

He didn't.

The fences at the Grand National are killers. Literally, on occasion. One of them, Becher's Brook, is considered the hardest obstacle in National Hunt racing – and you have to get over it twice, once as the sixth fence then again as the twenty-second. If you're going to fall at Aintree, you'll most likely do it at that fence.

Dream didn't fall. He navigated Becher's just as he navigated the course – skilfully as ever, but without, it seemed from the commentary, any real commitment to the cause. If a horse can be a Sunday driver, that was Dream. He just didn't seem interested. When he pulled up by the twenty-fourth I can't say it surprised me. What happened afterwards, however, did.

While the members of the syndicate and their myriad guests were swearing and tearing up their betting slips, I was only interested in getting to Tom. I wanted to know his opinion on Dream's performance. It just didn't seem right to me. He agreed. For the second race in succession he said, 'There was nothing in the tank.' Wilderness theory aside, that was unusual with so much time in between outings. The hard turf, the strangely clement weather, they were factors but not reasons. When I caught up with Philip I said, 'I think there's something wrong with him.'

Sometimes you don't enjoy being right. Philip arranged for tests and, while Dream sailed through most, one of them came back with a flag. As far as the vet could tell, our boy had burst a blood vessel during the race. His lungs had been filling up.

'What does that entail?' I asked.

'In layman's terms, he'd have been struggling for

oxygen so the harder he pushed, the more short of breath he'd got.'

Suddenly it all made sense.

'Do you think he's had this condition a while?'

'It's very likely,' they said. 'Severe stress can bring it on.'

When I thought of the big races, the ones where he'd gone beyond the pale, and the doldrums that followed, it all fell into place.

You poor boy, I thought. *The hell we've put you through when you weren't up to it.*

The 'wilderness' periods suddenly made so much sense. Whatever condition he had, it clearly manifested itself after a strenuous outing. It happened after the two wins at Chepstow and Haydock Park in 2006 and it happened again after his two big Exeter races. It happened after the run-in with Denman at the Hennessy and it was happening now. You can imagine how he must've felt because knowing Dream as I did, he would have been doing his best and I'm sure he must have felt very uncomfortable. Those times the jockeys had said he wasn't interested, he was very interested. He just couldn't do it. It wasn't that he lacked gas in the tank, he was missing oxygen in his blood. And we didn't know.

But now we did. Whatever caused the problem had been exacerbated by the weather and turf conditions at Aintree that day. If it had been wet and soft Dream almost certainly would have delivered. The harsher conditions took more out of them all. We'll never know for sure. All we could say for certain was that he had a condition which couldn't be ignored. To my mind there was only one way forward.

He has to retire.

Aintree 2010 was the last race Dream Alliance competed in. At least, that's what the record books should say in my opinion. But I was just one voice and, crucially, I wasn't a member of the Alliance Syndicate. They all heard the medical reports and they all had it put to them that Dream's condition prevented him performing in certain circumstances. It was also pointed out that if he retired immediately they'd have access to their share of the spoils. But they didn't bite.

'He's recovered from worse,' someone said. 'I say he'll do it again.'

'Why stick now when we could twist and earn even more?' said another.

The fact that Philip said the journalists and photographers at the Grand National had awarded Dream the title of 'Best Jumper at Becher's Brook 2009' just fuelled the flame. People were determined in their hope that there was more to come. So, when the vote came, it was decided that Dream would continue.

Whether he wanted to or not.

Sometimes people don't see the wood for the trees. I worried that was me. Was my desire to bring Dream home affecting my decision making? Because I'm not a rider, and I hadn't grown up with the beasts like Brian, I asked Philip, 'Would I be doing the horse an injustice by taking him home?'

He shook his head. 'On the contrary, Janet. Race-horses spend two thirds of their lives in the stable and for much of that they are hungry. Trust me, he will have a lovely retirement with you on your allotment.'

Sadly, that wouldn't be happening just yet.

I went along to Newbury on 27 November 2010 but I wasn't hopeful. Don't get me wrong, I wished Dream would ace the field. I just didn't think it was likely. And that, sadly, is how it transpired. It was a more than decent card, and even the mighty Denman only came third and Silver By Nature tenth. But our boy just wasn't up for it. Giles Hawkins had the command and by the sixteenth he knew Dream had had enough and pulled up.

Another 'PU' on the race card. *This is getting embarrassing*, I thought. *Please do the honourable thing and let the boy walk away.*

But no. There was a date in Dream's diary and it was with the Welsh National. For some reason it was held on 11 January 2011, but it could have been a year later and I suspect we'd have got the same result. Dream was one of nine previous course winners lining up, and I didn't rate our chances. To be honest, I wouldn't have fancied us against dogs. Tom O'Brien was once again the unfortunate fellow charged with squeezing the impossible out of a horse that wouldn't (in the syndicate's opinion) or couldn't (according to me) perform. When they eventually pulled up at the seventeenth I was screaming, 'That's enough. Let him go!'

But despite the *Racing Post* questioning whether it was time to call a halt on proceedings in their report, the syndicate was adamant: the journey must continue.

If our eminent trainer had been totally on board with the decision I'd have felt more comfortable. The truth is, Philip Hobbs was running out of ideas. Assuming the blood vessel injury wasn't permanently debilitating and it was mostly in the mind, he looked for every which way he could get a tune out of Dream. He tried everything to get him involved psychologically. And I mean *everything*.

He let him go hunting, they went chasing foxes, Philip even took him to the beach. He just wanted to get Dream engaged again mentally. He wanted him to regain the thrill of the chase. To actually *want* to run. It wasn't happening. There was no point entering him in yet another steeplechase where he'd not bother. If we were going to continue it called for a new strategy.

There was a cross country coming up at Cheltenham on 15 March so Philip put him in for that. It was the week before the famous festival so the world was still looking the other way. There was still a very healthy purse available to placed horses but honestly I couldn't see much of it coming our way.

And so it turned out. Tom was a mere spectator when Dream made a mistake at the second fence and repeated it at the third. They managed to get into a bit of a rhythm but it wasn't convincing. The race was long – thirty-two frightening fences – and at least he got round. But from the twenty-eighth it was obvious Dream had other things on his mind. When he came home eighth we actually considered that a decent result.

At least he finished.

There were plenty of people who took that result as a positive. I wasn't one of them. Neither, more importantly, was Philip.

'I have to be honest,' he said, 'but I don't think Dream wants to run any more.'

One of the reasons I like to go to Philip is because, as I've said before, he won't take your money for the sake of it. He'd already proved with Recurring Dream that he wouldn't take on your horse if he doesn't think it will race. It's no good for his reputation and it's no good for the horse. So when he said to us, 'There is no more I can do. I've done everything I can, the horse doesn't want to race any more,' that should have been the end of the matter.

But again, the vote went the other way. The syndicate decided that if Philip didn't want to stay involved they'd find a trainer who did.

'Perhaps,' Howard said, 'Dream would thrive under a smaller stable. He might benefit from closer attention.'

I didn't see any logic in this because to my mind no

stable was going to give us better care than Philip's. Just because Mr Hobbs himself wasn't hands-on personally with Dream every single day that didn't mean Dream wasn't being attended to with the utmost care. Johnson White and his team are the best in the business. But the syndicate had this fantasy that Dream would rise again, the romantic fools.

John Flint's name came up and when contacted he said that with a bit of TLC and hands-on care, Dream could be up and running – seriously running – in no time. I didn't believe it but Howard and enough others did. No offence to John, but in my opinion if Philip couldn't find a way then I didn't know a man on earth who could. That's the regard that I hold Philip Hobbs in.

I had nothing against John Flint as a trainer because I'd already moved Recurring Dream to his yard, although luck hadn't followed her. She'd had an accident on the gallops which resulted in the tendon over one knee randomly slipping. It was clearly painful and inoperable so running competitively was out of the question. According to Ron we couldn't breed from her either because the leg wouldn't take the extra weight. In the end he said, 'Considering the pain, my advice is to put her down.'

It was the hardest decision I ever took but for her own sake we did it. Whether she would ever have achieved anything over the jumps if she'd never got injured we'll never know. You get late bloomers with horses as much as people. Perhaps John would have got her flying eventually.

It was a horrible time. We still had Ianto coming through the system but he was the only positive. Dream Alliance was obviously treading water. It was simply a question of when the others would admit it.

Despite being against the move – or perhaps because of it – I remained a frequent visitor down at John's yard even after Recurring had gone. On the first occasion I could barely look at Dream.

'I know you don't want to be here and I'm doing my best to extricate you. But it might take time. Look after yourself till then.'

Guilt wasn't the only reason I'd gone. At the end of December 2010 my mother had passed away and, despite it not being a shock, I was knocked sideways. Over the next few weeks I'd have waves of blame and tears wash over me when I least expected it. They were hard to shake. Each time Brian said the same thing.

'Let's go and see the horse.'

Within two minutes of spilling my heart out to Dream I felt the weight lift from my shoulders and so I kept doing it even when he left Philip for John's. It never failed. I just wished I could have done the same for him. He wasn't going to win again. We both knew it.

'If I could get you out of here,' I said, 'I would. Just do your best and we'll be reunited soon enough.'

*

The first race under the John Flint banner was local. Very local, actually, round the corner at Ffos Las. The track is little more than a decent walk from our house but come 6 November 2011 I wish I hadn't bothered.

When we made our customary visit to the parade ring beforehand I couldn't look Dream in the eye. It was horrible. I felt guilty just being there. He was about to be put through something I didn't think he was up to. And he knew it, I could tell. What must he have thought of us? He knew he wasn't fit. He knew we knew. Horses aren't stupid. Dream certainly wasn't.

The going on the track was soft, there were only a dozen hurdles over nearly three miles, but there was only going to be one outcome. John's son Thomas was riding but I don't think A. P. McCoy could have done better. Despite some early pressing, Dream made a mistake at the ninth and by the next jump was nowhere. Ninth out of ten wasn't the result anyone wanted but it was the best we were going to get that day. Why couldn't anyone else see that?

Afterwards I couldn't speak to Howard, let alone Dream.

'That's it,' I said to Brian, 'I'm not going again. I can't watch this torture any more.'

On 31 December 2011, Dream ran at Warwick and came tenth out of fourteen. Back at Cheltenham for the cross country on 13 March 2012 he unseated Tom O'Brien. Then on 27 May they took him all the way to

Kelso in Scotland and he pulled up again. He didn't want to know.

I read all about this in the *Racing Post* online. As good as my word, I hadn't been to watch Dream race since Ffos Las. It gave me no pleasure being right. The only thing that would satisfy me at that stage was the syndicate recognizing it.

Finally, after Kelso, they did. Howard said they all had to admit that the end had arrived. I was happy for Dream but sad for my friend. This was a part of his life that Howard didn't want to end. Dream had given us all so much pleasure and I think he was hoping it could be reignited. But you can't reheat a soufflé. In the end, he and everyone else had to admit it.

Every cloud has a silver lining. When the syndicate finally called time on Dream's racing career I was so relieved. The boy was going to be put out of his misery. More importantly I hoped he was going to come back home to me.

As befits a syndicate, matters had to be wrapped up officially. I knew no minutes had been taken all that time ago at the first unofficial meeting but I wanted Brian to ask for Dream. There would be a vote of course, and then he would come home to the allotment. Just like I'd always planned.

When the final meeting came round I went along to watch. I couldn't bear the thought of losing Dream. If things went against me I didn't know what I would do. I charged Brian with the job of persuading the others. I might just as well have asked him to teach them French.

As the proceeding began I was beside myself with anxiety.

I waited and waited for Brian to ask for Dream before the vote was taken but he never did. It was decided by the syndicate that Dream should go to the stable lass who looked after him at Philip's. I couldn't believe what had happened.

In the car on the way back from the meeting, I turned on Brian.

'What happened?'

'I'm sorry.'

'Tell me why you didn't try to persuade them that I should have him. Tell me that.'

He looked at me like a rabbit in headlights.

'I was trying to protect you,' he said eventually.

'What from?'

It was like pulling teeth. He was my husband but it felt like I was trying to get my toddler son to admit he'd done something wrong.

'Couldn't you tell? There was a feeling in the room that now it's all over people didn't have to put up with you and me,' he said. 'If I'd asked for Dream to come to us I guarantee it would have been shot down by certain people and I didn't want to see it. I didn't want you to know that these people disliked us so much.'

It was a lot to take in.

'But we might have won the vote,' I said. 'Did you think about that?'

'We might have done but we'd also have discovered that several of the people we call friends were willing to stab us in the back. I'd rather not have that. I'd rather not sit there and listen to them slag you off.'

I could have throttled him. Did I mention I'm stubborn? I'd have sat there all night arguing. I'd have challenged the biggest of them to an arm wrestle to settle the matter. What I wouldn't have done is not put up a fight. In forty years of marriage I'd never felt the desire to walk away, but I felt it then.

'You've betrayed me,' I said. 'And you've betrayed Dream. I will never forgive you.'

It's only the harsh reality that I had nowhere else to go that prevented me from walking away that minute. If my parents had still been alive they'd have had me in their spare room. I really was determined to cut my losses and run.

The next morning I was calmer but only just. Brian's contrition, written all over his face, helped. But I couldn't accept it. Why would this stable lass get my horse?

I knew the girl well. I'd seen them both down at Sandhill so many times. Dream would be in good hands at hers, no doubt. But that wasn't the point. I got her number off Howard and rang. There was no answer so I sent a text.

'Look,' I said, 'I know you'll give Dream a good home, but I made him a promise, you see. I said that when his racing was over he'd come back to me. I'll pay for him if you like, I'll buy him, but I just want to honour my pledge. I owe him that.'

I never got a reply.

A few years later, while we were holidaying in Devon, Brian and I decided to call in to Dream's new home. It was lovely catching up with him. Clare, his new owner, couldn't have been nicer. Later on, we were asked to visit again as part of the TV programme *The One Show*. Clare made us welcome and said she was happy for us to come over whenever we wanted but the truth is, I found it too upsetting. There are only so many times you can walk away from someone you love.

Another outcome of the final Alliance Syndicate meeting was the sharing out of profits. During his career Dream Alliance had won £138,646 – with £97,839 coming from crossing the line first. After all the expenses and the experimental surgery, that meant a net payout to each member of £1,430.

It would have been less if Christine Brunnock had stayed on board but I would rather her have taken a share.

It wasn't an amount to change anyone's life but it was

a reminder. It said to me that dreams can come true. I wanted to breed a thoroughbred champion and, against all the odds, I did it. I reared a colt on an allotment built on a slag heap. I funded it with scraps from twenty-odd strangers. And I made it work.

If I never did anything else again, I knew one thing for sure. I was no longer Kelly's daughter, Trevor's sister or Daisy's wife. I was and am my own woman. I'm the person who did the impossible. And I did it by myself.

Epilogue

A Valleys Girl

Stepping out of the limousine into New York's Times Square was, I have to admit, not where I expected to be in 2015. But then I didn't expect to be attending the US premiere of a documentary made of my story. *Dark Horse*, written and directed by Louise Osmond, was a brilliant film about the life and career of Dream Alliance. She interviewed me, Brian, Howard and a few others from the syndicate, and cut it together with our personal videos and footage from TV races. The result was amazing. It wasn't just me who thought so. That year the film won Best Documentary at the British Independent Film Awards as well as Best Foreign Documentary at the Golden Trailers. It got nominated for a Critics' Choice award for Best Sports Documentary but the big one, the one that counts, was the Sundance Film Festival Audience Award.

After the premiere Brian and I had the option of going to Kentucky to watch the Derby. But you know what?

It's not true what they say. You *can* have too much of a good thing.

'I'd like to go home now please,' I said to the girl in charge of our itinerary.

'Are you sure?' she said. 'People would kill for this opportunity.'

'Let them have it then. Me, I'm a Valleys girl. All the world I need is back there.'

And I was right. You don't have to leave your village, let alone your country, to change the world. I've proved it and so can you. The future is out there. Don't let anyone or anything stand in your way. And if they do, remember the girl from the slag heaps who raised a champion.

Acknowledgements

This book and this story would not have been possible without my husband Brian, who always gave me the benefit of the doubt and helped me to follow my dream.

I also have to thank Howard for taking on the unpaid job of running our syndicate through all the ups and downs like a true dreamer, and Ron Williams, our vet. Ron brought Dream into the world and has been with us every step of the way. I could never have done it without him.

To the twenty-two owners/syndicate members that loved Dream enough to not give up on him, this is your story as much as mine.

To Philip and the whole team at Sandhill stables, for all the time and effort they put into Dream. I'm forever indebted.

To Judith and Louise, thank you for showing us off to the world in the documentary *Dark Horse*.

And finally, to David Riding, Jeff Hudson, Ingrid

Dream Horse

Connell, Charlotte Wright and everyone involved in the making of this book, thank you for caring so much about our beautiful superstar from the slag heaps of Wales.